Animal Rites

To Paul
who passed his first
test, with only a little
help from Emmanuella,
with flying colors.
KS

The Revd Professor Andrew Linzey is an Anglican priest and an internationally known theologian working in the area of Christianity and animals. He is a member of the Faculty of Theology in the University of Oxford and holds the world's first post in theology and animal welfare at Mansfield College, Oxford. From 1992-96 he was Special Professor of Theology at the University of Nottingham, and is currently Honorary Professor at the University of Birmingham and Special Professor at Saint Xavier University, Chicago. In 1998 he was appointed Visiting Professor at the Koret School of Veterinary Medicine at the Hebrew University of Jerusalem. He has written or edited twenty books including pioneering works on theology and animals: *Animal Rights* (1976), *Christianity and the Rights of Animals* (1987), *Animal Theology* (1994), and *Animal Gospel* (1998). *Animal Theology* has been translated into Spanish, Italian and Japanese. He is also co-editor of the *Dictionary of Ethics, Theology and Society* (1996) and of *Animals on the Agenda* (1998). He has lectured and broadcast extensively in Europe and in the United States, and, in 1990, he was awarded the Peaceable Kingdom Medal for outstanding work in the field of animals and theology.

Animal Rites

Liturgies of Animal Care

Andrew Linzey

SCM PRESS

Copyright © Andrew Linzey 1999

*Churches may reproduce single liturgies for one-off
services provided source and copyright are fully
acknowledged. For regular use or reproduction in
permanent form, permission in writing must first be
obtained from the publisher.*

0 334 02760 8

First published 1999
by SCM Press
9–17 St Albans Place, London N1 0NX

Second impression 1999

SCM Press is a division of
SCM-Canterbury Press Ltd

Typeset by Regent Typesetting, London
Printed in Great Britain by
Biddles Ltd, Guildford and King's Lynn

Contents

For Barney
still wagging his tail
in heaven

Introduction

Not a Sparrow Falls: Reclaiming Animal-Friendly Spirituality

At first sight the idea of praying for animals may appear a lost cause within Christianity. Almost nowhere in the common prayers and liturgies of the Christian church – for almost two millennia – do we find prayers for God's non-human creatures. There are liturgies which make some reference to creation, even some which boldly refer specifically to animals as such, albeit most usually in passing. But for the vast, if not overwhelming, majority of liturgical prayers offered by Christians, it is as though the world of animals was simply invisible.

Our prayers – or lack of them – say something about ourselves: our hopes, our concerns, our dreams for a better world, and most obviously the things we really care about. Do Christians then not really care about animals? Have they not seen the world of God's creation all around them teeming with millions of different forms of life? Have Christians not felt that these mysterious 'other worlds' also created by God merit some mention in our various prayerful offerings to the Almighty? Judged solely by its liturgical record, we might justifiably be led to a rather sad and firmly negative conclusion. It's not just that the crumbs are rather meagre; the liturgical cupboard is virtually bare.

No wonder then that prayers for animals appear an aberration. Thankfully, however, not all the prayers which

Christians offer to God – not to mention the wider contours of their spirituality – are recorded in common liturgies. The tradition which so firmly – at least in modern times – excludes animals is the same tradition which contains intimations of a wider, more animal-friendly spirituality.

II

Consider, for example, the witness of three notable saints of the Eastern Church of the fourth century: St Basil the Great, St Isaac the Syrian, and St John Chrysostom. It was St Basil who in his famous prayer entreated God to

> enlarge within us the sense of
> fellowship with all living things,
> our brothers the animals to whom you
> gave the earth as their home in
> common with us.

> We remember with shame that in the past
> we have exercised the high dominion
> of humans with ruthless cruelty
> so that the voice of the earth
> which should have gone up to you
> in song, has been a groan of travail.

> May we realize that they live not for
> us alone but for themselves and for
> you, and that they love the
> sweetness of life.[1]

What is remarkable is the way in which St Basil sets out and anticipates many of the central theological themes which were to dominate Christian thinking within the humanitarian movement over fifteen hundred years later: the celebration of creaturely fellowship based on the common origin of all creatures with God; opposition to cruelty as unjust and wrong in itself; the recognition – following St Paul – of the travail and suffering of fellow creatures, and last, but not least, the rejection of a wholly instrumentalist view of animals as simply here for us in favour of the recognition that they also live 'for themselves' and for God.

No less remarkable is the underlying vision of inclusive love provided by St Basil's contemporary, St Isaac the Syrian. He defines 'a charitable heart' as one without boundaries:

> It is a heart which is burning with love for the whole creation, for [humans], for the birds, for the beasts, for the demons – for all creatures. [Someone] who has such a heart cannot see or call to mind a creature without [their] eyes being filled with tears by reason of the immense compassion which seizes [their] heart; a heart which is softened and can no longer bear to see or learn from others of any suffering, even the smallest pain, being inflicted on a creature.

And St Isaac postulates this compassionate heart as the basis for prayer itself:

> That is why such a [person] never ceases to pray also for the animals ... that they may be preserved and purified. [This person] will even pray for the reptiles, moved by the infinite pity which reigns in the hearts of those who are becoming united with God.[2]

Lossky, in commentary, optimistically maintains that this 'cosmic awareness has *never been absent* from Eastern spirituality' and that in our way to 'union with God', humanity 'in no way leaves creatures aside, but gathers together in [its] love the whole cosmos disordered by sin, that it may at last be transfigured by grace'.[3]

Despite Lossky's fine words, the 'infinite pity' towards

animals, of which St Isaac spoke, *has* been lost in the subsequent prayers at least of the Western Church. Nowadays feeling for animals is not infrequently derided. But it was St Isaac's other great contemporary, St John Chrysostom, who could write with apparent assurance that: 'Holy people are most loving and gentle in their dealings with their fellows, and even with the lower animals.' And the rationale for this compassionate inclusivity is, according to Chrysostom, 'chiefly because they are of the same origin as ourselves'.[4]

In contrast then to the current narrowness of spiritual focus, we are able to locate powerful statements of concern for animals from some of the earliest celebrated figures within the Christian tradition. But are these intimations of prayer for, and care of, animals simply embellishments, albeit rather early ones, of a tradition which is otherwise fundamentally different or hostile? Have they in fact any dominical authority or christological grounding?

III

Since we know so little about the historical life of Jesus, it is hazardous to extrapolate from limited information. But the material in the Gospels is much more suggestive of animal-friendly concern than many have appreciated. One New Testament scholar, for example, has surveyed the evidence and concluded that Jesus 'clearly places himself within the Jewish ethical and legal tradition which held that God requires the people to treat their fellow creatures, the animals, with compassion and consideration'.[5] Among the various texts, there is one that has frequently been referred to but its full significance is rarely grasped. According to Luke 12.6, Jesus asks, 'Are not five sparrows sold for two pennies?', and responds, 'And not one of them is forgotten before God.'

The 'sparrows' in question are *strouthia*, the smallest kind of bird, regularly sold in the first-century Palestinian markets for the smallest amounts of money. In Jesus' day they were most likely sold for food, and in this context the saying of Jesus takes on new meaning. The very creatures bought and sold for next to nothing, are not 'forgotten' by the Creator. What is significant is the way in which Jesus points to the smallest sentient being commonly exploited for food, and widely regarded as an economic commodity, and declares its irreducible value to God. Richard Bauckham makes the logic clear: 'Jesus' arguments certainly presuppose that animals have intrinsic value for God. Otherwise it could make no sense to say that humans are more valuable.'[6]

More significant still is that the Jesus, recorded as indicating that even the smallest creatures are not forgotten by God, is the same Jesus who is later identified as the Logos, the Co-creator with the Father, through whom all things come to be. This is not the place to examine in detail the development of the doctrine in the history of early Christian thought (see, for example, Cochrane's *Christianity and Classical Culture*), but there are aspects of Logos doctrine that have implications for our understanding of animals. It is sometimes suggested that the Logos doctrine underlines the value and unity of the created world in Christ, and so it does, but might it also have specific and as yet largely unarticulated relevance to animals as well?

There are two key elements that need to be unearthed and explored afresh. The first is that the Logos becomes *flesh*. As C. F. D. Moule puts it: 'The Logos in St John is notoriously (and no doubt to the pagan reader shockingly) portrayed as having become flesh.'[7] But the flesh assumed in the incarnation is not some hermetically sealed, tightly differentiated human flesh; it is the same organic flesh and blood which we share with other mammalian creatures. There is no human embodiment totally unsimilar to the flesh of other sentient creatures. If this is true, it follows that God's Yes to flesh and blood is not just a Yes to undifferentiated 'life' as such, but a concrete and specific affirmation of the commonality of creaturely embodiment.

The second is that this fleshly existence affirmed in the incarnation is *sentient* existence, that is, sensitive flesh, vulnerable to injury and capable of suffering. From a theological perspective what distinguishes flesh is that it can be crucified. Here, I suspect, is the deep underlying theological connection between incarnation and atonement: the Word enfleshed *is* the Word crucified; the one is the necessary testament to the reality of the other. God does not become – in this sense – crucified flesh; God *is* the crucified flesh in our midst (for a brilliant exposition of this point, see Gray's 'The Myth of the Word Discarnate'). Again, there is a commonality between humans and animals necessarily presupposed here: animals are the similarly tortured and crucified flesh in our midst.

Once these connections are grasped, it becomes easier to understand the tradition of the saints and their extraordinary sense of kinship with, and care for, God's other fleshly creatures. Basil, Isaac, and Chrysostom do not stand alone. Saints as diverse as Guthlac of Crowland, Godric of Finchdale, Martin de Porres, Columba of Iona, Hugh of Lincoln, Catherine of Siena – and many others – by their words and deeds exhibited a practical understanding of the reality of kinship between all sentient beings established in the Logos. When, by the twelfth century, the tradition arguably reached its fullest flowering in the life of St Francis of Assisi, his biographer, St Bonaventure could sum up his theology in words that confidently reaffirmed Logos doctrine: 'When [St Francis] considered the primordial source of all things, he was filled with even more abundant piety, calling creatures, no matter how small, by the name of brother or sister, because he knew they had the same source as himself.' Moreover, it was Bonaventure who emphatically declared that 'every creature is by its nature a kind of effigy and likeness of the eternal Wisdom'. He entreats us:

Therefore, open your eyes,
alert the ears of your spirit,
open your lips
and apply your heart
so that in all creatures
you may see, hear, praise,
love and worship,
glorify and honour your God
lest the whole world
rise against you.[8]

It is difficult to dispute the authentic Christ-likeness of this tradition and its connection both implicitly in the teaching of Jesus and explicitly in subsequent christological doctrine.

IV

Between the thought of St Bonaventure and St Francis on one hand, and contemporary liturgy on the other, there has been such a colossal narrowing of concern that we may be at a loss to explain it. But account for it we must if we are to understand our contemporary spiritual poverty and find a way back to the fullness of the tradition. Four lines of explanation are possible.

In the first place, the saints and seers who so exhibited a sense of kinship with other creatures were rarely the theological systematizers and academicians who so increasingly made the running after the twelfth century, if not long before. St Francis was indeed honoured and revered, and lip service almost everywhere was paid to his name but his example – perhaps inevitably – never became the moral norm within christendom. More than that: his emphasis upon a wider kinship between all creatures came slowly but surely to be overtaken by the 'schoolmen' of theology – whose dominant emphasis was on rationality – and a particular kind at that.

Alec Whitehouse has described these thinkers as 'aristo-crats of the mind' whose primary impulse is to gain know-ledge through the exercise of analytical intelligence. Theologi-cal intuitions concerning the kinship of all creatures no matter how theologically or christologically sound could hardly win out against this mounting concentration on a par-ticular form of rationality – one which we now largely take for granted as almost the only form possible. But analytical or deductive reasoning is only *one* form of rationality. St Isaac himself spoke of another kind, which he described as 'simple cognition' or 'spiritual intellect' through which – according to Kallistos Ware – one 'understands eternal truth about God or about the *logoi* or inner essence of created things …'[9]

Moreover, not only did one form become dominant but also it was increasingly defined as the exclusive possession of human beings over and against the animal world. Hence a kind of pincer movement drove animals out of the realms of spirituality altogether, since the very spiritual capacities of human beings (most notably exercised through one form of reason) were those precisely denied to animals. Of course it needn't have been that way: humans could have so defined themselves whilst also maintaining the responsibilities of rationality towards the apparently non-rational. But it was not to be. The legacy is that the Christian tradition has enhanced and promulgated a version of rationality denied to animals and which in consequence has ensured that they ended up the moral and spiritual losers.

The second factor follows from the first. As Whitehouse puts it: 'Aristocrats of the mind are unwilling to be com-fortably or uncomfortably at home along with the world's minerals, vegetables, and animals.'[10] Once spirituality is defined in terms specifically and exclusively human, the non-rational others become otiose; the emphasis upon rationality displaces the commonality of flesh. Despite the lip service paid to the notion of the incarnation, Christian spirituality has historically been less and less concerned with embodied

8

existence, either human or animal, and much more with its renunciation.

Consider, for example, these lines from Jean Grou's *Manual for Interior Souls* published as late as 1892:

> This necessity of [carrying our cross] consists ... in separating our mind and heart from all terrestrial, carnal, and temporal objects, that we may occupy our thoughts and affections only with celestial, spiritual and eternal things; and to do this, we must struggle incessantly against the weight of our corrupt nature, which is always drawing us towards the earth. If we watch over ourselves, we shall constantly surprise in ourselves thoughts and desires which attach us to the earth, like animals, and which bring us back incessantly to the needs and well-being and the comfort of our bodies, and the means of procuring them. That which is physical occupies us far more than that which is moral, unless we make continual efforts to raise ourselves, as it were, above ourselves.

Note the underlying contrast between the 'spiritual' and the 'earthly'; especially the need to raise ourselves above thoughts and desires which threaten to attach us to the earth 'like animals'. Grou may have been extreme even for his time but it is one indication – among many – of what may be termed an 'otherworldliness' tendency which, perhaps unwittingly, denigrates other 'earthly' creatures.

Consider also this revealing line – ironically under the heading 'On the Dignity of Man': 'God loves poverty, crosses, humiliations, sufferings, everything that detaches us from the things of this life, and fixes our thoughts and affections upon future and eternal things.'[11] Such a blanket support of renunciation – whatever its wholesome (or as I fear rather unwholesome) results in other areas – inevitably had a knock-on effect in relation to animals. Given that animals are clearly earthly, and were frequently classified as 'things', we should not be surprised that intuitions concerning our fellowship with other 'things' have not been high on our spiritual agenda. One can only be rather amazed that 'detachment' and otherworldliness became such dominant motifs within a religious context so heavily indebted to a concept of incarnation.

The third line of explanation may be discerned in the firm distinction between the Creator and the created, and hence the traditional fear of idolatry. As I have pointed out elsewhere, Athanasius, despite his commitment to an indwelling Logos, was repulsed by those who 'applied the divine and transcendental title of God to stone or wood [or] ... irrational wild beasts, paying them full divine honours and rejecting the true and real God, the Father of Christ'.[12] Given the context in which some animals were apparently worshipped or deified, we should not be surprised by Athanasius' protest. But in the context of the tradition as a whole, it has left a lingering fear that any increase in the perceived moral and spiritual status of animals is a slippery slope to idolatry. Any liturgical focus on animals might have appeared like a concession to an alternative religious worldview. From an early point, Christians were marked out as those religious who did not worship animals.

If there has been any muddying of the waters here, it is certainly not the fault of modern-day animal advocates. For the one exception, of a qualified kind, that must be made to the above is the unusual twelfth-century cult of Saint Guinefort who was in fact a greyhound. According to legend, the dog saved a child from an attack by a serpent but was falsely accused and killed. A cult apparently grew up 'venerating the greyhound as a saint that could be called upon to protect children'.[13] Perhaps the main lesson to be learnt from this practice was that it so challenged the boundary between humans and animals that the Inquisition in the thirteenth century moved to stamp out the veneration.

The fourth explanation is related to the third. If liturgical interest in animals sounded like idolatry, no less so was its perceived threat to the primacy and uniqueness of humanity itself. Indeed among Christians who have opposed the whole notion of animal rights, there have been some who have not hesitated to argue that such thinking is in itself sub-Christian. Consider, for example, the statement of Tibor Machan that: 'If [humans] were uniquely important, that would mean that one could not assign any value to plants or non-humans apart from their relationship to human beings.' Machan's argument is of course a *non-sequitur* but it didn't stop the following lines of commentary by Joseph Kirwan:

> The root of the case for animals rights lies there. Its advocates do not believe that [humanity] is unique. That is why the notion of animal rights lies quite outside the Christian (or Jewish or Muslim) view of the world as God's creation and of [humanity's] place within it.[14]

Clearly Kirwan has not read my work and specifically my defence both of animal rights and also human uniqueness.[15] But that such false charges can be made are symptomatic of something much deeper within the Christian tradition. It is the sense that anything other than a wholly subordinate and instrumentalist understanding of animals fails to accord humanity its properly superior and unique role in the cosmos. So strong is this – what may be called a 'blik' – that I'm not sure rational argument can ever prevail against it. But its illogicality should at least be pointed out: to hold that animals deserve greater moral solicitude or that they have rights does not by itself dethrone humanity. As I have argued elsewhere:

> Some secular animal rightists, it is true, have argued in ways that appear to eclipse the uniqueness of humanity. But Christian animal rights advocates are not interested in dethroning humanity. On the contrary, the animal rights thesis requires the re-enthroning of humanity.

The key question is, What kind of king is to be re-enthroned? ... the kingly rule of which we are, according to Genesis, the vice-regents or representatives is not the brutalizing regime of a tyrant. Rather God elects humanity to represent and actualize the loving, divine will for all creatures. Humanity is the one species chosen to look after the cosmic garden (Gen. 2.15).[16]

What is most revealed in the arguments of those who appeal to notions of human 'uniqueness' is the frequent spiritual poverty of their understanding of that term. 'Uniqueness' has come to mean that other creatures are of little or no worth. But there is a deeper, christologically-informed, understanding possible: that our unique God-given privilege and power most authentically actualizes itself in care for the weak and defenceless. As Humphry Primatt once put it: '...the power granted unto [humans] to rule over the brutes cannot be a power to abuse or oppress them'.[17]

V

But the question may be asked: why animal rites? Even if the dominant emphases within the tradition have helped to obscure those of animal-friendly spirituality, how can the creation of specifically liturgical practices help us now?

The first answer to this question is that animal rites cannot by themselves rectify all the imbalances within the tradition. Animal rites cannot and do not stand alone. They are part of a small but increasing consciousness in theology, ethics and spirituality that animals merit theological time and attention. Animal rites in that sense is inseparable from animal theology, animal gospel, and even animal spirituality.

But it is doubtful whether these other spheres of activity can be properly accomplished without taking prayer for animals equally seriously. Christian life is not just about thinking, behaving, feeling, or praying, but all of these things. There is an integrity to Christian living which arises – can only arise – out of the pluriform nature of the activities which constitute its inner as well as outer life. That Christians do not liturgically bother much with animals is part and parcel of the wider neglect, both theological and ethical, of the well-being of animals.

There are certain things which liturgy can do which the other spheres of activity cannot. Specifically, there are some insights which require liturgical support in order to flourish at all. Take, for example, the notion that animals are creatures. This sounds a simple idea and Christians easily enough give nodding assent to it. But what is required spiritually is not just notional assent but the sustaining and development of this notion as a *perception*, as a way of seeing animals. What is desperately needed is to be able to *see* animals as God's creatures: to learn, and habituate ourselves to this perception, so that it becomes the primary or dominant lens through which we view animals every day. This is an immense spiritual task. It is also a deeply subversive one in a culture that thinks and speaks of animals largely in terms of machines, tools, commodities or resources. To be a Christian is – whatever else must be said – to be someone who *sees* animals as God's own creatures. This insight precisely because it is so foundational and fundamental – as well as counter-cultural – does not, cannot, survive without nurture and support. What liturgy can do is to set it on our spiritual agenda and thereby enable the process of personal discovery.

We 'learn' our faith through liturgy, that is, through the regular recital of words and the performance of actions which focus our deepest beliefs. Our beliefs also concern and affect our understanding of animals. To leave animals out of liturgy is to take them out of our spiritual cognizance of the world. It is to leave them where for the most part they still are: peripheral objects, marginal to our concerns, unrelated to our thinking about God the Creator. The old adage remains true: Christians are, what Christians pray. Even after almost two thousand years of Christian spirituality, we are only just beginning to learn what might be involved in describing animals as God's creatures. My New Testament scholarship may be all wrong, but I hazard a guess that what Jesus was implying by saying that God remembered even the smallest, cheapest birds in the market was that we would see (and do) it all differently if we really saw them as God sees them.

Allied to the issue of sustaining spiritual insight is the continuing need to take seriously what we have been regularly told is at the heart of our faith: the flesh. Consider, for example, these lines from Louis Bouyer in his defence of the relationship between 'natural rites' and Christian liturgy:

> [Humans] will thus come to realize that the originality of Christianity consists in consecrating their everyday lives through the Incarnation, and not in attempting to live in a world that is supposed to be holy but which is in fact artificial and out of contact with reality.
>
> The Incarnation, therefore, does not lead to the disappearance of natural sacredness but to its metamorphosis.
>
> The sacred is not so much a part of human experience as an aspect under which its entirety may be seen.[18]

Notice how Bouyer here repositions Christian spirituality against the 'otherworldly' tendencies within the tradition and argues that incarnational spirituality, far from being an escape from the world, must take seriously and build upon how we currently live in our 'natural' spheres of existence. The incarnation, from this perspective, is not about a flight from the world but a deeper engagement with it. If this line of apologetics is right, it must mean, *inter alia*, that our daily relations with other fleshly creatures must be brought into a much closer relationship with the God who becomes flesh in our midst.

Indeed, there is something distinctly odd, even perverse, about an incarnational spirituality that cannot celebrate our relations with other creatures. I am getting a little tired of theologians who are eager, sometimes over-eager, to see incarnational resonances within almost every area of human activity (art, music, poetry, dance) but who look with astonishment at the idea that our relations with animals might be an issue worthy of spiritual, nay incarnational, concern. I recall one eminent writer on spirituality who regularly spoke about the need to 'flesh out' the Gospel but when I questioned his eating habits could see no possible connection at all. This book will I trust 'flesh out' my critics and challenge them to extend the range of their otherwise admirable incarnational convictions beyond humanocentric parochialism.

Bouyer also questions the now established split between the sacred and the secular. Again if this position is correct, our 'secular' relations with animals, not least of all companion ones, acquire a new significance. There has been in recent years an increasing number of studies about the beneficial effects of keeping companion animals: how they help individuals to show affection, aid the growth of sensitivity in the young, and how they provide emotional support to the old. And yet despite the increasing acceptance of the therapeutic value of companion animals, there has been virtually no literature on the spiritual dimension of these relationships or any appreciation that these relationships may be spiritual at all (but see Webb, *On God and Dogs*, for a pioneering study).

Our spiritual blindness to animals – and our relations with them – has blunted our pastoral sensitivity as well. Clergy with few exceptions are the very people who cannot be approached with assurance by – for example – individuals who are suffering bereavement through the loss of a companion animal. Only a little while back, one leading church paper carried with amusement details of an occasion when a parish priest was asked by a parishioner for an appropriate liturgical means of marking the death of a much loved companion animal. The 'religion of the flesh', as Christianity has been described, is curiously unable to relate its incarnational theology to the real world of ordinary people who love their companion animals and who dare to think that a God of love might care for them too.

There is, then, a specifically pastoral need which this book attempts to address in the context of liturgy. For myself, I think that acknowledging an animal's life and marking its death are worthy liturgical aims regardless of whether humans are helped in the process. We owe the creatures and God their Creator at least that. But I am especially mindful of those believers for whom the lack of liturgical rites constitutes a continuing pastoral insensitivity: a failure to realize our emotional indebtedness to individual animals and to appreciate that in God's sight they count for something. The following pages are intended to offer creative ways in which the range of human emotions about animals can be channelled into a deeper appreciation that they too are God's creatures and that God's love affair with the flesh does not stop at the human species.

VI

I cannot overlook the fact that way back in 1976 I wrote *Animal Rights*, also published by SCM Press. It came out in the UK even before Peter Singer's now well-known *Animal Liberation* (Jonathan Cape 1976). My book pioneered the extension of rights language to animals and has in many ways heralded the modern animal rights movement. Back then, the notion of animal rights was still a novelty; now that the movement has grown and the ideas become more widely known, animal rights is deemed more threatening and controversial than ever before.

What, it may be asked, is the relationship between moral *rights* and liturgical *rites*? A number of theologians have entered the debate about animal rights by tripping at the first post. 'Rights is a secular discourse', they say; 'there are no such things as rights.' These responses have acted as a mental stop to thinking and prevented further investigation. It is vital that churchpeople and theologians move beyond these essentially facile reactions and begin some work of hermeneutics.

I say 'facile' because it is really too easy for Christians to label whole movements 'secular' and so avoid the challenges they represent. As I have argued elsewhere, the issue about rights is – demythologized – about moral limits.[19] To believe that a being has rights is to accept that there are moral limits to what we may do to it. The notion that there are such limits is a very ancient one. Many significant Greek thinkers from Pythagoras to Theophrastus have held and defended similar notions.[20] Indeed the Hebrew Bible is quite clear that there are limits to how far humans can exploit animals.[21] What rights language does quite deliberately is to present this very traditional notion in a sharp and challenging way. It helps us to see – what historically we have more often than not failed to see – that animals as individuals have very specific interests that we often leave out of account.

Put this way, it is not difficult to see that the animal rights movement actually builds upon the Judaeo-Christian tradition, and that far from being hostile to it (though of course it is rightly hostile to some Judaeo-Christian thinkers who have neglected animals) is deeply indebted to it. As I have argued elsewhere:

Animal advocates have not invented a world in which God makes us and all creation vegetarian; neither have they invented a world in which the lion lies down with the lamb. Both insights are given in the Judaeo-Christian tradition and rekindled afresh in a new generation. Far from modern advocacy diminishing biblical insights, in crucial respects it *depends* upon them.[22]

Some, I know, accept the foregoing but are still unhappy about the language of rights. But such language is capable of being construed in different ways (as it is in the movement itself) and has different theoretical bases. As I have subsequently defended the thesis, it has become clear to me that the issue of 'rights' is theologically about the rights of the Creator to have what is created treated with respect.[23] The strong language of rights is especially appropriate as a way of expressing *God's own* interest in the lives of sentient creatures.

Here, I think, is the underlying connection between rights and rites. The amazingly simple but profound truth that lies at the heart of this question both theologically and liturgically is the recognition that animals are *God's* creatures. They are not our property, they do not belong to us. Animals are not machines, resources, commodities, things, objects, tools, made for us or here for our use. Once this essentially theological discovery has been made there is no route back. What rites try to do liturgically are what rights try to do morally: to help us focus on *God's* creatures, beings with their own divinely-gifted value quite independent from their utility to us.

So the relationship between rites and rights is for me the relationship of the inner to the outer: the one seeking to demarcate limits of moral action and the other seeking to ritualize the spiritual vision of human-animal encounter which the tradition has, at its best, espoused. The rites, in other words, are the spiritual and liturgical in-working of the outer ethical sensitivity. If only theologians and Christians could see it, the animal rights movement is a displaced and currently unhomed *Christian* protest movement. At a time of distressing relativism in moral thinking, animal rights people are those holding out for a deontological account of our relations with the animal world. Animal advocates do not believe that we 'make-up' moral truth: they believe that we have to respond to (God-given) *loci* of value in the world.

All movements of ethical sensitivity have their rites. 'By their rites we shall know them' as Gerard Pottebaum has put it.[24] It is still not too late for the Christian community to develop and expand its rites so that its latent sensitivity can be manifest and in such a way that those who care for animals can identify the Christian vision of peacefulness as their own.

VII

There is no greater privilege than the writing of words that others may use to address God. But it is also an endeavour fraught with difficulties because of the increasingly fragmented and disputed nature of language itself. I am deeply sympathetic to feminist concerns that our language about ourselves and God bolsters up patriarchal and masculinist prejudices. Our whole way of writing up God has quite legitimately come under the moral hammer. Accordingly, I have worked assiduously to reduce and almost entirely eliminate masculinist language for God. Working mainly from the Revised Standard Version of the Bible because of its clarity and historical resonance, I have occasionally modernized its language while seeking to retain accuracy in translation. I have also taken the same liberty with one or two of the additional prayers and readings. The area in which I have clearly failed is in finding a plausible alternative to the central Christian metaphor of 'Father' and 'Son'; I can only hope that those who feel alienated will substitute their own vocabulary and endeavour to enlighten me on further usage.

In addition to the problem of masculinist terminology, I

have had to face the almost endemic nature of as yet only partly appreciated but (for some at least) no less alienating 'speciesist' language as well. That we have so few non-perjorative ways of speaking of animals should give us some pause. I have deleted as many 'beasts' and especially 'brutes' as I thought reasonable while appreciating that for pre-modern writers these words might not have carried the negative connotations they have for us today. Wherever possible I have used the word 'creature', since even 'animal' has become a term of abuse.

Our restricted vocabulary in both regards is a signal failure of our imagination within the tradition. What is desperately needed is a new language in which to express the range, complexity, and subtlety of our emotional interchange with animals, not to mention their spiritual status. We need to find new words borne of a new imaginative appreciation of the animal world in the sight of God.

This book is – to the best of my knowledge – the first of its kind in the world. I take no pride in this acknowledgment since it reflects so badly on the tradition. My hope is that those more skilled in liturgy and poetry (the latter I take to be the most desirable quality of all) will move on from my pioneering but modest efforts so that in years to come we shall have a wide range of liturgies available to the churches.

VIII

I owe a number of debts. Chief among these is to Joan Beth Clair's 1983 Master of Divinity dissertation from the Pacific School of Religion in Berkeley, California, entitled *Creature Rites*. Clair has the accolade of being the first in the world to do serious work on the theology and practice of animal-inclusive liturgies. Although I have not been able to follow all her radical revisioning of liturgy (including 'universalist eucharists' and 'baptism rituals' for non-human creatures), I am indebted to her work for inspiration and half the title of my book. I am also indebted to Margaret Lydamore of SCM Press for her courage in taking the project on and particularly for her words of encouragement when I was close to giving the book the last rites. My wife, Jo, generously typed, edited, and proofed the various drafts of the manuscript with her customary forbearance and patience.

My final word of thanks must go to the many hundreds of people who have written to me about the Service for Animal Welfare which I originally wrote for the RSPCA in 1975 and which has gone through five editions. Comments both kind and critical have helped me revise that project and prepare for this one. The test of any liturgy is of course in the praying, and I would therefore especially appreciate comments, suggestions, and feedback from individuals and communities who have used and prayed the following pages.

Andrew Linzey
Mansfield College, Oxford
11 September 1998

I

Celebrating the Creatures:
A Liturgy

There are few opportunities in contemporary Christian worship to celebrate our fellow creatures. That we go on worshipping as though the world of animals was invisible is a sign of a deep imbalance in our theology. More often than not, our worship reinforces and enhances the idea that God exclusively cares for the human species, or that only human beings can have a relationship with God. Christian worship in these ways actually diminishes both the activity of worship itself, and God as the object of our worship. For the God of Jacob, Isaac, Abraham and Jesus is not just interested in the human species and neither can the great themes of Christian preaching – creation, redemption and sanctification – be exhausted solely in relation to ourselves. That God loves and cares for all creation is the great lost truth of contemporary Christian theology and worship.

All the more extraordinary because there is ample biblical evidence that God does have a relationship with species other than our own. Many of the psalms – to take only one example – are replete with examples of how other creatures praise God. Indeed, according to Psalm 148, the praise of God begins in heaven and resounds throughout the entire creation. Worship and prayer, in this sense, are the activity begun by the Spirit to which we and all creation – though doubtless in differing ways – respond.

Karl Barth is not to be gainsaid on this matter. In answer to Calvin's question about what constitutes the supreme good, namely the knowledge of God, without which 'our condition is more unhappy that that of any of the brutes', Barth confidently asserts that 'brute beasts [sic] do (and the same can be said of the whole creation) accomplish God's intentions in creating them'. Moreover, the non-human, animate and inanimate, 'leave us [human beings] behind in the task of responding to their divine destination'. And how do we know this? Barth's reply is emphatic: 'Around us, praising is perpetual. The whole creation joins together in order to respond to God who created it. But ... [humanity] stands still and does not do what [it] should do. This is [humanity's] misery not to fulfil the meaning of [its] creation'.[1]

An attitude of inclusive celebration, of awe and wonder, is one that Christian worship desperately needs to recover. People who say that they have no need to go to church because they can better worship their Creator in the fields and woodlands are often making a much more serious point than perhaps even they appreciate. Many people do have an instinctive (for want of a better word) response of awe and wonder at the created world. Creation is not just 'out there' – a vast impersonal machine organized for our service. It is alive with the Creator Spirit. The lives of other creatures represent to us mysterious 'other worlds' of God's creativity; it is the response of faith that wants to stand awestruck at the wondrous works of God.

Celebration is also essential if we are to have a proper regard for animals as our fellow creatures. As I have written elsewhere:

... there is a direct relationship between our inability to celebrate animals and our dismal record of exploitation. We should not be surprised if we exploit our fellow creatures if we do not know how to celebrate, rejoice, and give thanks for the beautiful world God has made. If we treat the world as trash it may be because so many people imagine the world as just that.[2]

Celebrating the Creatures: A Liturgy

The theological basis for our celebration should now be obvious: we rejoice because God the Creator rejoices. Specifically the complex God of Father, Son and Holy Spirit delights in differentiated creation: in its wonderful variety, complexity and magnificence.

What follows is a short liturgy which tries to express and focus some of these lost ideas within the Christian tradition. Of course the doctrine of creation does not stand alone: what is created will also be redeemed, and creation for all its greatness is not yet finished. One cautionary note therefore seems essential. In celebrating creation we must not make the mistake (as sadly some eco-theologians still do) of deifying it. Creation is not God. Neither can it be read as a moral text book. We celebrate what is good in creation without thinking it all universally or absolutely good. Much damage has been done to a theological understanding of animals by the simple assertion that 'nature is God's will' or at least unambiguously so.[3] Creation is ambiguous because it is – in traditional terms – 'fallen', that is, incomplete, and, at least to some extent, at variance with the original will of its Creator.[4]

Our celebration of creation therefore requires (as I hope I have at least partly achieved) a strong hint of eschatology. We celebrate creation and our fellow creatures, and mirror (we hope) God's own rejoicing but we do so looking to the consummation of all things in Christ. We need always to remember that our fellow creatures – blessed and enlivened by God's Spirit – not only respond to and praise their Creator but also sigh and groan, awaiting with us, the new creation in Christ.

Priest   We have come together to rejoice with God the Creator at the wonderful creation around us.

O God, you love all things that exist: and despise none of the things which you have made, for you

would have made nothing you didn't love. You
spare all things, for they are yours – O Lord who
loves the living. For your immortal Spirit is in all
things.
(Wis. 11.24–5, 26–12.1)

All   Let us sing to the Lord
a new song:
a song for all the creatures
of the earth.

Priest   Let us rejoice
in the goodness of God
shown in the beauty
of little things.

All   Let us marvel
at the little creatures
who are innocent
in God's sight.

Priest   Let us extol
God's handiwork
in the complexity
of their lives.

All   Let us not be haughty or proud
too full of ourselves
to praise the Lord
of little things.

Priest   Let us rejoice
in the other worlds
sublime and mysterious
that God has made:

All   the world of earthworms
burrowing in the ground;

Priest   the world of skylarks
soaring above us;

All   the world of foxes
playing around their dens.

Priest   Let us hear
the divine rejoicing
throughout the whole earth:
'the earth is mine
and the fullness thereof'.
(Ps. 24.1)

First   O Lord, how manifold are your works!
Reading In wisdom you have made them all;
the earth is full of your creatures.
When you open your hand
they are filled with good things.
When you hide your face
they are dismayed;
when you take away their breath
they die and return to their dust.
When you send forth your Spirit
they are created;
and you renew the face of the ground.
(Ps. 104.24, 28b–30, RSV)

All   Help us to wonder, Lord
to stand in awe;
to stand and stare;
and so to praise you
for the richness of the world
you have laid before us.

Animal Rites

Priest God of the universe
all creatures praise you:

the sun setting on the lake,
the birds flying upward toward the heavens;

the growl of the bear,
the darting of the stickleback;

the purring of the cat,
the wide eyes of the tiger;

the swift legs of the cheetah,
the dance of the hare;

the lapping of the dog,
the descent of the dove.

God of a thousand ears
the music of your creatures
resounds throughout creation
and in heaven a symphony is made.

All Help us to wonder, Lord
to stand in awe;
to stand and stare;
and so to praise you
for the richness of the world
you have laid before us.

Second [The Logos] extends [its] power everywhere,
Reading illuminating all things visible and invisible,
containing and enclosing them in [itself], [giving]
life and everything, everywhere, to each
individually and to all together creating an
exquisite single euphonious harmony.[i]

There follows a period of silence

All   Christ in all things
restore our senses
and give us again
that experience of joy
in all created things.

Priest   Christ in all things:
in the waves breaking on the shore;
in the beauty of the sunset;
in the fragrant blossom of Spring;
in the music that makes our hearts dance;
in the kisses of embracing love;
in the cries of the innocent.

All   Christ in all things
restore our senses
and give us again
that experience of joy
in all created things.

There follows a period of silence

Priest   Large and immense God
help us to know the littleness
of our lives without you;
the littleness of our thoughts
without your inspiration;
and the littleness of our hearts
without your love;

you are God beyond our littleness
yet in one tiny space and time
you became one with us
and all those specks of dust
you love for all eternity;

enlarge our hearts and minds
to reverence all living things
and in our care for them
to become big with your grace
and signs of your kingdom.

A prayer to God the Holy Spirit

Heavenly dove
descend on us
we pray
and in your flight
reunite our sinful wills
to your heavenly will
so we may soar upwards
and see the smallness
of ourselves
amid the vastness
of your unfolding creation.
Amen.

All   We look forward
with all your creatures
to the wonderful consummation
of all things in Christ
when death and pain
shall be no more
and the whole earth
shall unite with those
in heaven and
praise your name
saying:

Worthy are you
our Lord and God
to receive glory

and honour and power
for you created all things
and by your will
they were created
and have their being.
(Rev. 4.11)

Priest   God of manifold blessings,
source of all
that is good
and true and holy,
raise us up to see
the world through your eyes
so that we may treasure
each blessed creature
alive with your Spirit
and touched by your creative hand;
and may the blessing of
this wonderful God
Creator, Redeemer and Sanctifier
be upon us
now and forever,
Amen.

---

i St Athanasius

2

A Service for Animal Welfare

What follows is a revised and adapted version of the Order of Service for Animal Welfare I originally wrote for the RSPCA in 1975. Since publication it has gone through five subsequent editions and has sold thousands of copies. It continues to be used by hundreds of churches which hold annual 'animal blessing services' mainly, though not exclusively, in the United Kingdom. Services are usually held on 4 October which is World Day for Animals and also the Feast Day of St Francis of Assisi.

Some may be surprised to learn that an animal welfare organization such as the RSPCA should be publishing distinctly Christian, indeed liturgical, material. Few appreciate that the RSPCA itself came into existence as a direct result of Christian vision. The Society was founded by an Anglican priest, Arthur Broome, who called together the first meeting which led to the Society's foundation in June 1824. Broome's work was immensely sacrificial. He gave up his London living to work full-time (unpaid) for the Society as its first Secretary and ended up in prison because of the Society's debts. The first Minute Book records the declaration that 'the proceedings of this Society are entirely based on the Christian Faith and on Christian Principles'.[1] The first prospectus, penned by Broome himself, makes clear its Christian inspiration:

Our country is distinguished by the number and variety of its benevolent institutions ... all breathing the pure spirit of Christian charity ... But shall we stop here? Is the moral circle perfect so long as any power of doing good remains? Or can the infliction of cruelty on any being which the Almighty has endued with feelings of pain and pleasure consist with genuine and true benevolence?[2]

The emphasis in the founding documents on the extension of 'charity' and 'benevolence' is theologically significant. Against scholastic theology which then – as now – was uneasy or hostile to the extension of duties to animals, the new Society constituted a protest movement.[3] Often without knowing it, those who work for animal welfare are heirs to one of the most successful Christian protest movements in the Western world.

This service champions the notion pioneered by Broome and others – and still represented by the continuing work of the Society – that the powerful have a special duty to protect the weak – indeed that it is 'the vocation of the strong to be gentle'. What I have elsewhere described as 'the Christ-given paradigm of lordship expressed in service' and inclusive moral generosity.[4] At their best such services provide an opportunity to espouse Christ-like care for animals, to preach about Christian responsibility, and to rekindle a sense of creaturely fraternity and fellowship.

Some precautions are essential if animals are to be brought into church. Great care must obviously be taken to avoid any distress to the animals themselves. Fresh drinking water should always be available, and animals should not be placed alongside other species with whom they have a natural antipathy. If the animals are to be blessed, they should be brought individually to the front of the church.

Despite some organizational difficulties (usually very minor) the bringing of animals into church has a deep symbolic importance – one that is seldom lost on the human participants. It symbolizes the inclusion of the animal world into the very place where so much theology has excluded them. It also provides a practical glimpse of creation in praise.

Animal Rites

One or more of the following sentences may be said

In the beginning God created the heavens and the earth. *(Gen. 1.1)*

And God saw that everything was made, and behold it was very good. *(Gen. 1.31)*

I will remember my covenant which is between me and you and every living creature of all flesh. *(Gen. 9.15)*

O Lord, you save both humans and animals. *(Ps. 36.6)*

They shall not hurt nor destroy in all my holy mountain; for the earth shall be full of the knowledge of the Lord as the waters cover the sea. *(Isa. 11.9)*

Are not five sparrows sold for two pennies? And not one of them is forgotten before God. *(Luke 12.6)*

The creation itself will be set free from its bondage to decay and obtain the glorious liberty of the children of God. *(Rom. 8.19–21)*

Priest Almighty God
we come together
to thank you
for the beauty and glory of your creation;
to praise you
for your holiness and grace;
to acknowledge our responsibility to animals
and for our use of the created world.

But, first of all, we pray for your forgiveness
because of our part in sins of thoughtlessness
and cruelty towards animal life.

A pause for reflection may follow

All   Almighty God
you have given us
temporary lordship
of your beautiful creation.
But we have misused our power,
turned away from responsibility
and marred your image in us.

Forgive us, true Lord,
especially for our callousness
and cruelty to animals.

Help us to follow the way
of your Son, Jesus Christ,
who expressed power in humility
and lordship in loving service.
Enable us, by your Spirit,
to walk in newness of life,
healing injury, avoiding wrong
and making peace with all your creatures.

Priest   God of everlasting love,
who is eternally forgiving:
pardon and restore us,
and make us one with you
in your new creation.
Amen.

First Reading
Either (a) In the beginning God created the heavens and the
earth. The earth was without form and void, and

the darkness was upon the face of the deep; and the Spirit of God was moving over the face of the waters.

And God said, 'Let the earth bring forth living creatures according to their kind: cattle and creeping things and animals of the earth according to their kinds.' And it was so.

And God said, 'Behold I have given you every plant yielding seed which is upon the face of the earth, and every tree with seed in its fruit; and you shall have them for food. And to every animal of the earth, everything that has the breath of life, I have given every green plant for food.' And it was so. And God saw everything that was made, and behold, it was very good.
(*Gen. 1.1–2, 24–26, 29–31a, RSV*)

or (b)   The wolf shall dwell with the lamb,
and the leopard shall lie down with the kid,
and the calf and the lion and the fatling together,
and a little child shall lead them.

The cow and the bear shall feed;
their young shall lie down together,
and the lion shall eat straw like an ox.

The suckling child shall play
over the hole of the asp,
and the weaned child shall
put his hand on the adder's den.
They shall not hurt or destroy
in all my holy mountain;
for the earth shall be full
of the knowledge of the Lord
as the waters cover the sea.
(*Isa. 11.6–9, RSV*)

A Service for Animal Welfare

The following may be said or sung

All   All praise be yours thru Brother Wolf,
All praise be yours thru Sister Whale,
By Nature's son my Lord be praised,
By Brother Eagle, Sister Loon.
Thru Sister Flower, Brother Tree.
Let Creatures all give thanks to Thee.
All praise to those who live in peace.[i]

Second Reading

Either (a) I consider that the sufferings
of this present time
are not worth comparing
with the glory
that is to be revealed to us.
For the creation waits with eager longing
for the revealing of the sons of God;
for the creation was subject to futility,
not of its own will
but by the one who
subjected it in hope;
because the creation itself will be set free
from its bondage to decay,
and obtain the glorious liberty
of the children of God.
We know that the whole creation
has been groaning in travail
together until now.
(Rom. 8.18–23)

or (b) [St Francis] rejoiced in all the works of the hand
of the Lord and saw behind all things pleasant to
behold their life-giving reason and cause. In
beautiful things he saw Beauty itself, all things

were to him good. '[The One] who made us is
the best,' they cried out to him.

He embraced all things with a rapture of unheard
of devotion, speaking to them of the Lord and
admonishing them to [offer] praise. He forbade
the brothers to cut down the whole tree when
they cut wood, so that it might have hope of
sprouting again. He commanded the gardener to
leave the border around the garden undug, so
that in their proper times the greenness of the
grass and the beauty of the flowers might
announce the beauty of the Father of all things.

He removed from the road little worms, lest they
be crushed under foot; and he ordered that honey
and the best wines be set out for the bees, lest
they perish from want in the cold winter. He
called all animals by the name 'brother' [or
'sister'], though among all kinds of animals he
preferred the gentle. For that original goodness
that will one day be all things and in all, was
already shown forth in this saint as all things in
all.[ii]

*There follows an address or sermon on some aspect of
Christian responsibility for the created world. (Suggested
text: 'The righteous care for their animals, but the wicked are
cruel', Prov. 12.10)*

*The following litany may be said or one of the other litanies
on pp. 78–90*

Priest   Let us pray with the whole church and in the
            words of its saints, poets and theologians for all
            those who struggle against the abuse of animals
            and for the rebirth of compassion in our hearts:

Every creature is by its nature a kind of effigy
and likeness of the eternal Wisdom.[iii]

Reader   Almighty God, we pray for grace to perceive
your creative hand in all things.

Priest   Lord in your mercy

All   Hear our prayer.

Priest   We praise Thee, O God, for Thy glory displayed
in all the creatures of the earth. For all things
exist only as seen by Thee, only as known by
Thee.[iv]

Reader   Help us, O God, to be full of praise for all your
creatures.

Priest   Lord in your mercy

All   Hear our prayer.

Priest   Surely we ought to show kindness and gentleness
to animals for many reasons and chiefly because
they are of the same origin as ourselves.[v]

Reader   Increase in us, O God, a sense of fellowship with
all your creatures. Help us to walk humbly and
tread gently on your good earth.

Priest   Lord in your mercy

All   Hear our prayer.

Priest   What is a charitable heart? It is a heart which is
burning with love for the whole creation ... a

heart which can no longer bear to see or learn from others of any suffering, even the smallest pain, being inflicted on a creature.[vi]

Reader   Almighty God, we pray for loving sensitive hearts towards all your creatures.

Priest   Lord in your mercy

All   Hear our prayer.

Priest   A robin redbreast in a cage
Puts all heaven in a rage.[vii]

Reader   Help us, O God, to set animals free from our own cruelty and greed.

Priest   Lord in your mercy

All   Hear our prayer.

Priest   I was early convinced in my mind that true religion consisted in an inward life, wherein the heart doth love and reverence God the Creator and learn to exercise true justice and goodness not only toward all [people] but also toward the [animal] creatures.[viii]

Reader   Dear God, help us to recover humility in our relations with animals and to realize that it is the vocation of the strong to be gentle.

Priest   Lord in your mercy

All   Hear our prayer.

A Service for Animal Welfare

Priest	It must be remembered that we are required to practice justice even in our dealings with animals.[ix]
Reader	Almighty God, help us to deal justly with animals, living without wantonness and promoting kindness.
Priest	Lord in your mercy
All	Hear our prayer.
Priest	Almighty God, we give thanks for all those who have gone before us and given us examples of courage, mercy and faith.
All	Lord of all life your creation groans in travail awaiting the glorious liberty of the children of God; by your Spirit help us to free creation from its bondage, to heal its pain and obtain that liberty which is your gift to all creatures. Amen.

Animals are now brought to the front of the church and they are blessed individually by the priest

This or one of the other forms of blessing (pp. 102–107) may be used

Priest	May God Almighty Father, Son and Holy Spirit

bless this creature
protect it from cruelty
and grant it
a share in the redemption
of the world.
Amen.

One or more of the following prayers may be said

Priest   Heavenly Father,
your Holy Spirit
gives breath to all living things;
renew us by the same Spirit
that we may learn to respect
what you have given
and care for what you have made,
through Jesus Christ
your Son, our Lord.
Amen.

Almighty God
your Son, Jesus Christ
taught us to love
even the least among us,
give us the courage to care
for all living creatures
and the strength to defend
even the weakest of all.
Amen.

Holy Father,
your Son, Jesus Christ
is the reconciler of all things
in heaven and on earth;
send us your Spirit
that we may be made one
with all your creatures,

and know that all things
come from you,
and belong to you,
now and forever.
Amen.

The general blessing may now be given

Priest   Eternal Father, by your power of love you cause
all things to be, strengthen by the merciful
example of your Son, Jesus Christ, all those who
struggle and work for the alleviation of suffering,
prosper their endeavours by the power of your
Holy Spirit; and may the blessing of God
Almighty, Creator, Redeemer and Sanctifier, be
upon you and remain with you always.

All   Amen.

---

i   Scott Winter
ii   Celano, *Francis of Assisi*
iii   St Bonaventure (1221–74)
iv   T.S. Eliot (1888–1965)
v   St John Chrysostom (c.347–407)
vi   St Isaac the Syrian (c.347–438)
vii   William Blake (1757–1827)
viii   John Woolman (1720–72)
ix   John Calvin (1509–64)

3

Eucharistic Prayers for All Creatures

Thanksgiving is at the heart of Christian worship, and the great eucharistic prayers provide an opportunity to remember and recollect the saving works of God in creation, incarnation and redemption. As such it is the natural place to give thanks for what God has given in creation – and, not least of all, to remember the millions of other species that God has made. And in some of the earliest forms of eucharistic prayers known to us, there are explicit references to the creation of animals.

For example, in the seventh book of the early Apostolic Constitutions the 'craftsmanlike Wisdom' of the Creator is extolled which 'does not neglect to provide for [the animals'] divers needs any more than it failed to produce their diversity'.[1] Indeed the same prayer speaks of the 'eucharist for all things' offered by humanity on behalf of all creation in anticipation of the universal Sabbath, defined as nothing less than the 'repose of creation' and the 'fulfilment of the world'.[2]

It is this idea of the 'eucharist for all things' that has inspired the following four eucharistic prayers which like some of their earliest forerunners specifically include mention of other living creatures. The idea that humanity should specifically represent the rest of creation – especially in worship – is not of course new. The theology of the Eastern Church, especially in the thought of St Maximus, has frequently viewed humanity as a 'microcosm' of the entire creation.[3] In contrast Western eucharistic rites have been – to say the least – sparing in their allusions to the animal world.

44

There is something especially fitting about the idea that humanity should represent other creatures and in so doing exercise a priestly role in creation, if, that is, our priestly role is understood as 'a participation in God's redeeming presence in the world'.[4]

We need to regain an appreciation of the eucharist as a foretaste of the realized kingdom. As E. L. Mascall puts it, the eucharist 'is not only the sacramental and eschatalogical representation of the redeemed community; it is also the sacramental and eschatalogical representation of the restored and transfigured universe'.[5] Thus the bread and the wine are symbols of an entire creation lost and found in Christ.

First Eucharistic Prayer

Priest   The Spirit of the Lord is with us

All   And with all creation.

Priest   Let us praise our Creator

All   And give thanks for the wonderful earth.

Priest   Let us sing a song of praise with the whole creation

All   Let everything that has breath praise the Lord.

Priest   Lord and heavenly Father
in your hands
you hold heaven and earth;

all things proceed from your creative will
for you have made each creature
perfect in itself as a sign of your eternal grace;

and yet humankind has corrupted your purpose
turning from light to darkness
and releasing evil in the world.

What you once gave us
has lost its innocence
through our sin
and been marred by our selfishness;

even so you have not despaired of us
but sent your Son
to rescue us and all creation
from the abyss of suffering and death;

yet still we resist your saving work
and frustrate your Spirit within us

and so we pray that this same Spirit
will today renew us and set us right
with ourselves and all creatures.

The priest takes the bread and wine into his or her hands and says

Holy Father
accept these gifts of bread and wine
symbols of creation lost and found
in your Son
and send your Holy Spirit
upon them so that they may be to us
the body and blood of your Son
who transforms each and every particle
of creation
with your love.

We remember when Jesus took bread
and said 'This is my body'
and gave the cup of wine
and said 'This is my blood'.

May this food be for us
a foretaste of your heavenly kingdom
in which all creation
shall be redeemed by your grace
and our selfish wills
transformed by your holy will.

Filled with this hope
and your grace
we offer you
holy Creator
Lord of all
Saviour of the universe
our song of thanksgiving
and join with all creatures
in these words of eternal praise:

All   Holy, Holy, Holy
Lord God Almighty
heaven and earth
are full of your glory
now and for ever.
Amen.

Second Eucharistic Prayer

Priest Spirit of the living God be upon us

All   And all the creatures of the earth.

Priest Let us be filled with the Spirit of thanksgiving

All   And let all creation praise you.

Priest Yours, Holy Father,
is the Word

spoken at the beginning
through whom all things
came to be;

this is the Word
source of all creation
who gives life
to all creatures;

this is the Word
that became enfleshed in history
speaking to us
through flesh and blood
and in works of love;

this is the Word
that became our suffering
nailed on a tree
for our liberation;

this is the Word
that still speaks
through your Spirit;
invites us to love
and care for all creatures.

*The priest takes the bread and wine into his or her hands
and says*

By the power
of God's Spirit
may the Word
which became flesh
become to us
flesh and blood
in this bread and cup
symbols of all creation
united and perfected

in the same Word
spoken through
all eternity.

Christ
the incarnate Word
took the bread
and said
'This is my body'
and he took the cup
and said
'This is my blood'.

In this act
all creation
is spoken for
by the Word;
everything existing
is offered to the Father
and not one crumb
of the gift of life
is lost or falls away.

Holy Father
the Word
you have become
has set us free
to love, forgive and care;
let us now with these gifts
of bread and wine
live our freedom
for the sake of
all creatures
and in your name
minister to them as
your Word
ministers to us.

We join our words
with the one Word
of love
and in thanksgiving
and praise
we sing:

All   God beyond the heavens
all that lives is yours
and in your Word
shall all be made one
now and for all eternity.
Amen.

Third Eucharistic Prayer

Priest   The Spirit of God's justice is upon us

All   And all the creatures of the earth.

Priest   God's Spirit is creating a new heart among us

All   We shall feel again God's Spirit within us.

Priest   God's Spirit is liberating us from injustice

All   The whole creation awaits the liberty of the
children of God.

Priest   God of justice
your Spirit
sends the prophets
among us
but we have not
heard them;

Isaiah spoke of
the future peace
in which the lion and the lamb
shall dwell together
but we have chosen
the way of violence;

Hosea spoke of your
covenant established between all living things
but we have abused the
kinship between all creatures;

Amos declared your judgment
against the greedy and cruel
but we have exploited
your earth;

your Son gave us an example
of sacrificial love
reflecting your self-giving
to the world
but we crucified him
and still crucify others.

Even then
you did not leave us
without witnesses
to your grace:

St Chrysostom said
holy people are
kind and loving
to all living beings;

St Francis called
all creatures
brothers and sisters
and rejoiced in them;

Margery Kempe saw
your crucified Son
in the suffering
of children and animals.

We have rejected
these voices
but still you send
your prophets among us:

John Wesley preached
the redemption of
all creatures in Christ;

Cardinal Newman saw
the Christ-like innocence
of all defenceless creatures;

Arthur Broome sacrificed
his life for the
crusade against cruelty;

Albert Schweitzer taught
reverence for life
as a necessity of thought.

God of justice
in each generation
your Spirit sends
us your prophets of peace;

help us to honour
those who speak in your name
and preach your gospel to all creatures.

*The priest takes the bread and wine into his or her hands
and says*

God of justice
this is the sacrament of our liberation

given for us and all creation
as a sign of your coming kingdom.

At the last supper
before his final act of sacrifice
your Son, Jesus Christ,
took the bread and said 'This is my body'.
He took the cup and said 'This is my blood'.

May these creaturely gifts
of bread and wine
be to us the body and blood
of your Son
who died to establish your
justice on earth
as it is in heaven;

and as we eat and drink
these holy things
we pray for grace
that we may become
prophetic signs
of that holy justice
for which all creatures long.
Amen.

In thanksgiving we pray
the words of Mother Julian of Norwich:

All   All shall be well, and all shall be well
and all manner of things shall be well.

The whole creation awaits your eternal Sabbath
O Lord, when all creatures shall be free
and your justice shall fill the earth
as the waters cover the sea.

Liberating God: Father, Son and Holy Spirit,
we praise you forever. Amen.

Fourth Eucharistic Prayer

Priest   The Spirit of life is upon us

All   who gives breath to all creatures.

Priest   The Spirit is moving on the face of the earth

All   and we feel the Spirit in our hearts.

Priest   The Spirit is renewing us

All   and all the creatures on the earth.

Priest   Holy Father
your Spirit fashioned us
from the beginning
created us from the dust of the ground
and breathed upon us;

and all creation too
was enlivened by your Spirit
free and abroad in all creation
making life by your work of love.

Nothing living is untouched
by your Spirit or without
your gift of grace;

the earth is full of your treasures
great and small are the works of your hands;

everywhere we behold your glory
and the superabundance of your Spirit;

by the same Spirit
we are moulded together
into one fellowship of life;

such is your pattern
that everything speaks of you
and every speck of dust
is transfused with glory.

You set us in the midst of life
to care and serve;
to walk humbly with you
and trust in your Spirit;

but we have betrayed that trust
and have served ourselves
worshipping our own image
and frustrating your Spirit within us;

only your Son
filled with the Spirit
has set us free
and liberated us
to walk again
in newness of life;

yet the Spirit of your Son
still cries in our hearts
so that all creation
may be free again with your love.

*The priest takes the bread and wine into his or her hands
and says*

Through your same creative Spirit
we pray that these
creatures of bread and wine
may be to us
the very life of your Son
in flesh and blood;
signs of life renewed
for the whole creation.

At the last supper
Jesus took bread and
said 'This is my body'
and he took the cup of wine
and said 'This is my blood'.

As we remember
your Son's saving work
we pray that you will
remember us and all creation
when we come into your kingdom.

All   Driven by the same Spirit
we confess you, Lord of Life,
source of all that is good,
beautiful and true
and we commit ourselves
to that life of care
manifest in your Son, Jesus Christ.

Lead us Holy Spirit
to the place of
our hearts
where we shall see and know
the living God;
and find in that place
a world of life,
always praising
always joyful
singing together:

Holy, Holy, Holy
you are the true life
without end and for evermore.
Amen.

4

Covenanting with Animals: A Liturgy

Modern theology has almost entirely neglected the biblical insight that God's covenant extends not only to human beings but also to all living creatures. In the work of Karl Barth – to take just one example – notice is taken of the inclusivity of the covenant but the idea is then practically disregarded.[1] This liturgy is an attempt to redress the balance: to provide an opportunity for the renewal of the covenant between ourselves and other creatures, especially those companion animals who share our lives.

Strictly speaking, it is not 'our' covenant but God's own covenant. We do not create such a relationship; rather we find ourselves placed in such by the Creator. What this liturgy does is to draw out the moral and spiritual dimensions implicit in the fact of the covenant relationship itself, and invite human response.

It is especially important that this should be done in relation to companion animals. Companion animals are entirely dependent upon us and wholly subject to our control. They would not, in most cases, exist at all if it were not for us. This concentration of power requires an explicit and public acceptance of responsibility. In Christian terms, all power exercised without responsibility is akin to the demonic. Churches could take the lead in helping 'owners' to understand that we do not, properly speaking, 'own' animals at all; they are first and foremost creatures of God. When we co-opt animals into our lives, especially when they are used

*and enjoyed for companionship and love, we create relation-
ships of dependence and trust which incur heavy responsibility. Despite the (understandable) popularity of companion
animals among children, they are actually an adult responsibility.*

*Baptist preacher Charles Spurgeon once recounted the
view of Rowland Hill that a person 'was not a true Christian
if his [or her] dog or cat were not the better off for it'. And
commented: 'That witness is true.'² In the same spirit,
churches have an opportunity to signal in their liturgy the
spiritual import of our relations with companion animals.
Domestication has, to say the least, been a mixed blessing for
the animals concerned. Many are still badly and cruelly
treated (indeed records for cruelty to domestic animals are at
an all time high in the UK), innumerable 'pets' are neglected,
abandoned and discarded after purchase like consumer items.
Indeed, more than a thousand 'unwanted' dogs are destroyed
each week in the UK. Given this context, encouraging a right
relationship with animals wholly at our mercy is a Christian
duty.*

*People who keep animals have often made an elementary
but profound discovery: animals are not machines or commodities but beings with their own God-given life (nephesh),
individuality and personality. At their best, relations with
companion animals can help us to grow in mutuality, self-
giving, and trust. Indeed, one recent theologian has boldly,
and in my view rightly, suggested that in these relationships
of apparent 'excess' we see prefigured and actualized nothing
less than the self-giving of God. 'I want to suggest that, from
a theological perspective that takes pets seriously, animals are
more like gifts than something owned, giving us more than
we expect and thus obliging us to return their gifts.'³ Far from
decrying these relationships as 'sentimental', 'unbalanced', or
'obsessive' (as frequently happens today), churches could
point us to their underlying theological significance – as living
examples of divine grace.*

Covenanting with Animals: A Liturgy

Some may argue that the covenant here celebrated is rather one-sided; there is strictly speaking no 'contract', and hence the use of the covenant motif is inappropriate. In fact, no person who has had any affective relations with companion animals could suppose for a moment that the relationship is wholly one-sided. But it is true that, if not one-sided, they are largely initiated from one side. And here, most surely, we properly mirror God's own covenant with ourselves and all other creatures. The initiative, at least, is all God's, and that for all of us should be a source of joy.

One or more of the following sentences may be read

> God formed out of the ground all the wild animals and all the birds of heaven. God brought them to the man to see what he could call them, and whatever the man called each living creature, that was its name. *(Gen. 2.19, NEB)*

> I will remember my covenant which is between me and you and every living creature of all flesh. *(Gen. 9.15, RSV)*

> And I will make for you a covenant on that day with the beasts of the field, the birds of the air, and the creeping things of the ground; and I will abolish the bow, the sword, and war from the land; and I will make you lie down in safety. *(Hos. 2.18, RSV)*

Priest   Holy God
you have established your
covenant with us
and with our
future generations;
despite our fecklessness

and sinfulness
you have bound yourself
to us;

despite our violence
you have promised
a covenant of peace;

despite our infidelity
you have remained
faithful to us;

but not only
with ourselves
but with all
living creatures
is your covenant established:

creatures that walk
on the ground;
birds that fly
in the air;
and creeping things
that move along
the earth;

all these creatures
you have bound
to yourself in
faithfulness
and love.

Truly, you are
a remarkable God
whose graciousness
knows no limits
and before whom
no creature is
left desolate

or bereft of
your grace;

not only have you
created the great earth
but also you are to
each and every creature
their kind and loving God;

everything living looks
to you for their
sustenance and care;
without you, all the
creatures of the earth
would perish.

All   All these living creatures
you have put under our protection
and we are to care for them
as you care for us;

but we know that
we have often treated
creatures in our power
wantonly, selfishly
and thoughtlessly;

we have thought
of them only as objects
for our amusement and pleasure;
we have neglected their true needs;
we have betrayed your trust.

Pause for reflection

For these sins
gracious God
we are truly sorry;

we ask your pardon
and forgiveness.

Priest   May God the Creator
accept your
repentance and
grant you forgiveness.

All   Mindful of the great
responsibility you have placed
upon us, we now renew our
covenant with these creatures
in our care, and pray that
we may be faithful to them
as you are faithful to us.

May the unity of peace
which you have established
between all species
never be broken by
our violence

and may our lives
reflect that generosity
of spirit which we
see manifest in your
Son, Jesus Christ.

Priest   God of unity and peace
send us now
your Holy Spirit
that we may feel
a deeper kinship
with all living creatures
and by this act of renewal
reaffirm the bond of covenant
with these animals in our care.

Covenanting with Animals: A Liturgy

Each animal is brought individually to the front of the church and the priest asks these questions of its human companion

Priest	Will you name this creature?
Respondent	*(The name of the animal is given)*
Priest	Will you care for (*Name*) as God's own creature?
Respondent	I will with God's grace.
Priest	Will you be mindful of *his/her* Christ-like vulnerability?
Respondent	I will be so mindful.
Priest	Will you love and protect (*Name*) so long as *he/she* lives?
Respondent	I will with God's grace.
Priest	Will you be faithful and kind in good times and bad?
Respondent	I promise to be so faithful.

The human companion is invited to touch/pat/stroke the animal as a sign of the covenant reaffirmed between them

Then the priest says

> May the God
> of the new covenant
> of Jesus Christ

grant you grace
to fulfil
your promise
and to show
mercy to other creatures
as God has
shown mercy
to you.
Amen.

Reading   Put on, then, garments that suit God's chosen
and beloved people: compassion, kindness,
humility, gentleness, patience. Finally to bind
everything together and complete the whole there
must be love. Let Christ's peace be arbiter in
your decisions, the peace to which you are called
as members of a single body. Always be thankful.
Let the Gospel of Christ dwell among you. Let
every word and action, everything you do, be in
the name of the Lord Jesus, and give thanks
through him to God the Father.
(Col. 3.12, 14–16a, 17, REB)

All   Eternal Father
we thank you
for these creatures
who live alongside us
as our companions and friends;
for their loyalty, love
and trust which enrich
our lives and give us joy;
teach us
the value of kindness
the power of mercy
the strength of gentleness;

and create in us
a new spirit of humility
in the face of your creatures
within whose covenant
they live and die;

we ask these prayers
through your Son
Jesus Christ
whose new covenant
of love
gives life
to us all.
Amen.

5

Liturgies for the Healing of Animals

The idea that Christian ministry ought to extend to healing sick animals is not quite as new as it sounds. There are innumerable stories, admittedly all apocryphal, of Jesus or his disciples befriending and protecting animals. One of the most revealing is found in the Gospel of Pseudo-Matthew *(eighth century) which pictures the young Jesus playing with lion whelps, and admonishing them to 'Go in peace and hurt no one, neither let [humans] injure you ...'[1] Less fantastic and possibly more authentic is a Coptic fragment which recounts a story of Jesus healing a mule beaten by its owner. The periocope ends with a familiar sounding admonition: '... from now on do not beat it any more, so that you too may find mercy'.[2] Whatever their precise authenticity, both are indications that, at some point in the tradition, Jesus' ministry was understood to be inclusive of animals.*

There are at least a couple of hints that these stories or embellishments find a starting point in the canonical portraits of Jesus. In the synoptic Gospels, Jesus is represented, at least implicitly, as accepting that rescuing an animal fallen into a pit even on the Sabbath is a religious duty.[3] To which needs to be added the strange verse in Mark 1. 13 where Jesus is pictured as beginning his ministry 'with the wild beasts'.[4] Allied to this are the dramatic examples of the many saints who protect, befriend, and also heal suffering animals directly. St David Garesja – to take just one example – apparently defended the partridge which hunters had come to kill with these confident words: 'You can kill neither me nor the partridge for my God is with me and [God] is powerful to protect.'⁵

Moreover, there appear to be some authorized prayers for animals. The Rituale Romanum, for example, contains this blessing for sick animals:

> We humbly seek thy pity, O Lord; that these animals, which are troubled with a grievous infirmity, may be healed through thy name and by the strength of thy blessing. May all diabolic power be annulled in them, and may they be no longer ill. Be Thou to them, O Lord, the defender of their life and the restorer of their health. ⁶

Nevertheless, it remains true that there are no authorized healing liturgies for animals anywhere in the world. It is difficult to judge this as anything other than an omission. That healing is pre-eminently a Christian work is beyond dispute. And, more glaringly still, it is hard to see any theological grounds for supposing that Christ's world-transforming ministry of reconciliation excludes other suffering creatures. In my view, then, we can and should suppose that the healing of any suffering is a divine, or rather Christ-like, work and, if so, there is good reason to embody this attitude in liturgical practice. For what liturgy does is to focus the offering, the service of the church in the name of Christ for the healing of the world. The churches may have forgotten suffering animals but we can be sure that God the Creator – whose mercy extends to all creatures – has not.

More even than that: there is something profoundly Christ-like about the innocent suffering of creatures who have done no harm and who are utterly dependent upon our mercies. In my view, the innocent and the most vulnerable, such as young children and animals, make a special moral claim upon us. They are, in other words, paradimatic cases, even litmus tests of our Christian compassion.

First Liturgy

Priest   The God who comes to us in Jesus Christ is a God of healing and redemption whose purpose is to reconcile all things through the Son.

In him all the fullness of God was pleased to dwell, and through him to reconcile to himself all things, whether on earth or in heaven, making peace by the blood of the cross.
(Col. 1.20, RSV)

For anyone united to Christ, there is a new creation: the old order has gone; a new order has already begun. All this has been the work of God. [God] has reconciled us through Christ, and has enlisted us in this ministry of reconciliation.
(II Cor. 5.17–18 REB)

God of the universe
without boundaries
of race, creed, colour or species
in whose sight every life is precious;

we know that you have entrusted us
with your ministry of reconciliation;

may your transforming power
break through into our
disordered and violent world
so that we may become the means
through which
your kingdom is proclaimed
and the sick healed.

There follows a period of silence after which the following prayer is said by the congregation

All   Send us your Holy Spirit
            that we may be agents of
            your healing and reconciling power
            for these suffering creatures.

*The animals are brought individually to the front of the
church*

*The priest, together with one or more members of the
congregation, lays hands on them and says*

            May Jesus Christ
            reconciler of all things
            heal and restore you.

            May the healing power of
            the living Christ
            deliver you from
            all affliction.

            In the name of Jesus Christ
            I bring you healing
            and peace.

If holy oil is to be used, the following prayer may be said

            May this be to you
            a sign of Christ's
            healing and transforming
            power.

*After the laying on of hands there follows a period of
silence*

Then the following prayer is said by the congregation

All   Holy Father
            as your Son

ministered to us
in works of love
enable us to
minister to these
suffering creatures
and by our deeds
proclaim your
gospel to all creation.
Amen.

Priest   Eternal Father
in the Cross of your Son
you identified yourself
with the weak, vulnerable
and innocent
who suffer in our world,
expand and enlarge
our compassion for
all creatures who suffer
and by your Spirit
strengthen those who care
even for the
least of all
through Jesus Christ
our Lord.
Amen.

May God
the reconciler of all things
before whom nothing is unloved
and no life is forgotten
make you agents of Christ's peace;
and the blessing of God Almighty,
Father, Son and Holy Spirit
be upon you
now and for ever.
Amen.

Second Liturgy

Priest   God's own Son
Jesus Christ
was given to us
for the healing
of the world.

We know that the whole
creation groans in pain
awaiting its
final liberation
in Christ.

Let us pray in quiet for
the Holy Spirit
that the healing power
of Christ
may be manifest among us.

There follows a period of silence

All   As your Son
outstretched his hands
to bless and to heal,
so we believe,
Holy Father,
that your Spirit
is alive among us
giving us power to
overcome suffering
and transform
evil into good;

we pray
that you will
look with compassion

on these your
suffering creatures
and grant that
our ministering hands
may be your means
of healing
in a broken world.

*Each animal is brought individually to the front of the
church*

*The priest and others who are to lay hands on them say
together*

We do as Christ did:
we use our hands to
bless and heal
in the name of the
one God,
Father, Son and Holy Spirit.
Amen.

*As the priest and one or more members of the congregation
lay hands on each animal, one or more of the following
prayers may be said*

May the healing power
of the living God,
Father, Son and Holy Spirit,
be upon you.
Amen.

May Jesus Christ
Son of the living God
heal and preserve you.
Amen.

Liturgies for the Healing of Animals

If holy oil is to be used the following prayer may also be said

> May this holy oil
> be a sign of the
> healing presence of
> the risen Christ.
> Amen.

After the laying on of hands there follows a period of silence and then the congregation says

All   Holy Father
turn your face
we pray
towards these
suffering creatures
and by the
power of your Spirit
may your
healing love
descend upon them
through Jesus Christ
your Son, our Lord.
Amen.

Priest   Healing and transforming God
whose face is seen in the
suffering of your Son;
be present with these creatures
and prepare us all
for that final transfiguration
when all suffering shall be
transformed into joy
and your kingdom shall reign
on earth as in heaven.

May the blessing of God Almighty
Father, Son and Holy Spirit
be upon these creatures
and all who care for them
now, this day, and for evermore.
Amen.

Third Liturgy

Priest   We have come together
to proclaim the work of
Christ our liberator:
the very agent of God
who abolishes death;
heals the sick;
identifies with the outcast;
defends the vulnerable;
cares for the poor;
frees us from evil;
and inaugurates a kingdom
of peace and justice
for all creatures.

All   Blessed be the God
who liberates us
and all creation
from suffering and injustice.

Priest   As Christ cared for the human poor
and despised, so we must
care for those in our power
and especially our fellow creatures
abused and tortured in our midst.

Especially we pray for
these innocent animals

who suffer through no fault
of their own and for whom
Christ also died.

All Compassionate God
   fill us with your power
   to do good;
   may your hands which
   have healed us
   be the same hands
   through which we
   in your name
   heal and succour
   these innocent creatures.

After a period of silence the following prayer is said

All May the Spirit
   of the liberating Christ
   be upon us
   and free us to do
   his work of love
   in an unloving world.

Animals are brought individually to the front of the church

*The priest and one or more members of the congregation
lay hands on each animal using one or more of the
following sentences*

  Christ the healer
  liberate you from pain.

  Christ the redeemer
  restore you to health.

  Christ the new creature
  make you whole.

Animal Rites

There follows a period of silence
Then the priest says

        Christ our Liberator
        you know the prisons
        of our hearts
        and how our compassion
        for other creatures
        is shrunken and pathetic
        in your sight:
        give us Christ-like courage
        to defend the weak and the vulnerable,
        and make us strong
        in mercy and generosity
        to advance God's justice
        until the end of our time on earth.

All   Christ the peacemaker
        bring us peace;
        Christ the compassionate
        give us compassion;
        Christ the just
        lead us to justice.
        Amen.

6

Litanies for Animal Protection

Despite the theological problems associated with petitionary or intercessory prayer, it remains true that the prayer that Jesus taught is almost entirely petitionary in character. If praying that God's will 'be done on earth as it is in heaven' is pre-eminently the Christian prayer, then there can be no good reason not to pray that God's will be done in relation to the animal world specifically.

Our prayer, then, should be that God's suffering creatures will be healed, that we will turn away from our wanton exploitation of animals, and that we will repent of our arrogance and spiritual blindness. It will be seen in the following litanies that I think our prayer should equally be for our – as well as the animals' – liberation. I have used elsewhere Jonathan Edwards' image of the Fall as a state of shrunken human sensibilities – a state in which we become less and less sensible to other creatures and more and more obsessed with ourselves.[1] From this perspective, our mal-treatment of animals – and our desire to see them and treat them as objects or commodities – stems from a spiritual poverty and hardness of heart. We need, in short, to find a new heart for animals.

We should pray for this new heart: this sensibility, this feel-ing for animals. For some it comes naturally but for most of us, it does not. In my view, feeling what is now rather per-joratively called 'pity' should be a goal of our spiritual life. Even if we cannot scale the heights of the spiritual sensibility exhibited by the saints, at least we ought to feel a lack of it: a sense of unwholeness, and pray for the grace to feel.

Animal Rites

*I like the lines from Charles Péguy that we pray to be
'spared from becoming a dead people, a dead nation'. He
continues: 'Be spared from mildew. Be spared from going
rotten in spiritual death, in the earth, in hell.'* [2] *Ecclestone, in
commentary, suggests that the contrary words – not of death
but of life – 'are being spoken wherever men and women go
that extra mile as "burden-bearers of creation", taking it on
themselves to make some acts of reparation and reconciliation or giving themselves generously to patient service of
others'.* [3] *These thoughts have inspired the following three
litanies.*

First Litany

Priest   Our prayer is that the God of the new covenant
written into our hearts will enlarge our sense of
kinship and fellowship with all living beings.

One or more of the following sentences may be said

Create in me a clean heart, O God; and renew a
right spirit within me. *(Ps. 51.10)*

Search me, O God, and know my heart: try me,
and know my thoughts. *(Ps. 139.23)*

And I will give them a heart to know me, that I
am the Lord; and they shall be my people, and I
will be their God; for they shall return unto me
with their whole heart. *(Jer. 24.7)*

A new heart also will I give you, and a new spirit
will I put within you; and I will take away the
stony heart out of your flesh, and I will give you
a heart of flesh. *(Ezek. 36.26)*

This is the covenant I will make with them after those days, says the Lord. I will put my laws into their hearts, and in their minds will I write them. *(Heb. 10.16)*

Passionate God
we are cold
with hearts of stone;
we are deaf to the cries
of your creatures
and blind to their sufferings.

Warm us with your Spirit
so we can feel your passion
raging against injustice
and burning away evil.

Bring us
out of the cold
from our passionless lives
to the heat of your love.

There follows a pause for reflection

Priest	For animals neglected and ill-treated
All	Give us new hearts, O God.
Priest	For animals hunted to death
All	Give us new hearts, O God.
Priest	For animals exhibited for entertainment
All	Give us new hearts, O God.
Priest	For animals killed for convenience

All	Give us new hearts, O God.
Priest	For animals in crates and tethers
All	Give us new hearts, O God.
Priest	For animals genetically manipulated
All	Give us new hearts, O God.
Priest	For animals bought and sold in markets
All	Give us new hearts, O God.
Priest	For animals suffering in laboratories
All	Give us new hearts, O God.
Priest	For animals patented as inventions
All	Give us new hearts, O God.
Priest	For animals slaughtered for food
All	Give us new hearts, O God.

Priest   O God
give us new hearts
that we may feel again
the suffering of our
fellow creatures;

deliver us
from ourselves
and the evil
we inflict
on the animal world.

Litanies for Animal Protection

There follows a pause for reflection

Priest	From our denigration of animals
All	Free us, O Lord.
Priest	From thinking of animals as things
All	Free us, O Lord.
Priest	From our indifference to cruelty
All	Free us, O Lord.
Priest	From our systematic exploitation of animals
All	Free us, O Lord.
Priest	From treating animals as machines
All	Free us, O Lord.
Priest	From our abdication of responsibility
All	Free us, O Lord.
Priest	From our spiritual blindness
All	Free us, O Lord.
Priest	From our shrunken sensibilities
All	Free us, O Lord.
Priest	From our hardness of heart
All	Free us, O Lord.

Priest   Liberating God
release us from that
spiritual poverty
that sees other creatures
only as commodities for us
and reduces them to things
for our service.

Holy God
you alone
can make all things new;
send your Holy Spirit
upon us;
give us new hearts to feel,
new ears to hear,
new eyes to see
the unity of
all creatures
in Christ;
and to proclaim
all living beings
as fellow creatures
with us in your
wonderful creation.
Amen.

Second Litany

Priest   God of flesh and blood
whose Son Jesus Christ
died in agony on the Cross;
help us to hear the cries
of our fellow creatures
who suffer and die
for our sakes.

Litanies for Animal Protection

All   We confess our faith in the true God:

Priest   This is the true God

All   Who comes to us in the flesh.

Priest   This is the true God

All   Who suffers in the suffering of the world.

Priest   This is the true God

All   Whose face is seen in the faces of pain in our
           world.

Priest   Merciful God
           help us to
           see that there is
           something profoundly
           Christ-like about
           the innocent
           suffering of animals;
           give us grace
           to feel with you
           their pain
           and so to share
           the burden of suffering
           which lies
           upon the world.

           O God who will free
           all creation from evil,
           deliver us, we pray,
           from our own
           spiritual poverty
           so that by your grace

we may become
new creatures in Christ
alive with your Spirit.

There follows a pause for reflection

Priest   From our hardness of heart

All   Deliver us, O Lord.

Priest   From our littleness of love

All   Deliver us, O Lord.

Priest   From our lack of care

All   Deliver us, O Lord.

Priest   From our greed and cruelty

All   Deliver us, O Lord.

Priest   From our wanton killing

All   Deliver us, O Lord.

Priest   From our desire to dominate and control

All   Deliver us, O Lord.

Priest   From our overweening pride

All   Deliver us, O Lord.

Priest   From our contempt for other lives

All	Deliver us, O Lord.
Priest	From our lack of shame
All	Deliver us, O Lord.
Priest	From our inability to repent
All	Deliver us, O Lord.
Priest	From our obsession with ourselves
All	Deliver us, O Lord.
Priest	From our sense of self-satisfaction
All	Deliver us, O Lord.
Priest	From every desire to inflict harm
All	Deliver us, O Lord.
Priest	From every form of violence
All	Deliver us, O Lord.

Priest   Fill us, O God, with sorrow for the suffering we have inflicted on the animal world; take from us our conceit and pride and give us true humility in our dealings with animals; help us to see through our excuses and rationalizations for our cruelty, and to repent of the evil we have done them. We ask these prayers through your Son, Jesus Christ, who on the Cross identified with all those who suffer and in whose name shall all creation find liberation and fulfilment. Amen.

May the God
who turns
us from evil,
who endures suffering
for our sake,
and who forgives
all who are penitent
grant you lasting
forgiveness that
you may become signs
of light in a
dark world.
Amen.

Third Litany

Priest   We confess our belief in the Triune God, Creator,
Reconciler and Sanctifier who loves each and
every creature.

All   This we believe and know:
animals are our fellow creatures
loved by God the Father
redeemed by God the Son
and enlivened by God the Holy Spirit.

Priest   Holy Trinity
awaken within us
a sense of feeling
for all the living creatures
you have placed among us;
give us a compassionate heart
for all who suffer
and make us visible signs
of your peaceful kingdom
for which all creation longs.

Litanies for Animal Protection

God of justice and peace
you hear the cries
of all your creatures:

hear our prayer for
all our fellow creatures that are

imprisoned in zoos

All   and let your mercy be upon them;

Priest   transported overseas

All   and let your mercy be upon them;

Priest   hunted for sport

All   and let your mercy be upon them;

Priest   exploited in circuses

All   and let your mercy be upon them;

Priest   dissected in schools

All   and let your mercy be upon them;

Priest   abused in laboratories

All   and let your mercy be upon them;

Priest   forced into factory farms

All   and let your mercy be upon them;

Priest   butchered in abbatoirs

All   and let your mercy be upon them;

Priest   trapped for their fur

All   and let your mercy be upon them.

Priest   Merciful God
we are made in your image
but we have made gods of ourselves;

we have turned your creatures
into things and machines,

making them objects of our sport
using them for our vanity,
exploiting them for our greed
and stealing their lives;

but you are the Liberating God
who can transform
even ourselves;

help us to turn from
our evil
and embrace
the vision
of your peaceable
kingdom:

They shall not hurt nor destroy
in all my holy mountain;
for the earth shall be full
of the knowledge of the Lord
as the waters cover the sea.
(Isa. 11.9, RSV)

There follows a pause for reflection

Priest   From our lack of vision

All   Liberate us, O God.

Litanies for Animal Protection

Priest   From our self-centred lives

All   Liberate us, O God.

Priest   From our lack of pity and compassion

All   Liberate us, O God.

Priest   From our idolatry of ourselves

All   Liberate us, O God.

Priest   From our callousness to suffering

All   Liberate us, O God.

Priest   From our lack of humility

All   Liberate us, O God.

Priest   From our arrogance and pride

All   Liberate us, O God.

Priest   From our violent, disordered lives

All   Liberate us, O God.

Priest   Liberate us, O God, from the folly that sees all creatures as simply resources, machines, or commodities here for our sake. Help us to understand that all living creatures are precious in your sight and exist for your glory.

    Make us sorry for the continuing crucifixion we inflict on the animal world; of your mercy forgive

us, and enable us by your Spirit to lead lives
worthy of our repentance: in the name of the
same God, Creator, Reconciler and Sanctifier
who redeems each and every creature and whose
kingdom is everlasting peace. Amen.

7

A Vigil for All Suffering Creatures

The very least that can be said about vigils is that they try to keep us awake – no mean feat since they are usually held at night time when our natural inclination is to sleep. They derive their biblical inspiration from the story of Jesus in the Garden of Gethsemane when he asked his disciples to 'watch and pray' (Matt. 26.41). Although vigils have been kept for a variety of purposes throughout Christian history, they are now an increasing rarity. Indeed, all except that for Easter were abolished by the Roman Catholic Church in 1969.

The spiritual value of vigils lies in the sense of wakefulness, alertness and watchfulness which they can – at best – engender within us. They enable us, in other words, to cultivate a spirit of attentiveness. It is precisely this capacity which we need in relation to the suffering of animals. So much of the suffering that animals undergo is unattended, unnoticed, unremarked, in fact hidden away in laboratories, abbatoirs, or factory farms. In order to think theologically and spiritually about animals we have first and foremost to attend to them, and that requires space, and more often, practice.

In what follows, I relate the suffering of animals to Christ's own suffering and passion. It will be seen that I entirely support the recent tendency within theology to emphasize the suffering of God – not least of all as a correction to earlier presentations of God as so transcendent as to be unconcerned about earthly misery. If, as I believe, the doctrine of the Cross reveals a God intimately involved in the suffering of the world, there can be no good theological grounds for excluding sentient animals from its scope and meaning.

Few have so well grasped the Christ-like innocence and suffering of animals as John Henry Newman in his remarkable sermon on Good Friday in 1842 – a passage from which is included for meditation in the vigil that follows. Taking up the scriptural image of Christ as the Lamb, he posits the moral equivalence of the suffering inflicted on Christ to that inflicted on innocent animals. He concludes: 'Think then, my brethren, of your feelings at cruelty practised on brute animals, and you will gain one sort of feeling which the history of Christ's Cross and Passion ought to excite within you.'[1]

If we attend to animal suffering in this context and with these eyes, we shall be rewarded with a deepened understanding both of christology and creaturely suffering. For Christians of all people whose eyes are fixed on the innocent suffering of the Crucified ought to be sensitized to the innocent suffering of fellow creatures. That given, I have also dared to spell out my conviction that to stand for Christ must mean standing against the many contemporary practices which inflict suffering on animals.

A large crucifix is placed on the altar or table and a candle is lit

Priest   The crucified Jesus is the only accurate picture of God the world has ever seen.[i]

All   Let us meditate on the truth of the Cross of Christ.

Pause for reflection

Priest   God defines himself when he identifies himself with the dead Jesus.[ii]

All   Let us meditate on the truth of the Cross of Christ.

Pause for reflection

Priest   God has made the suffering of the world his own in the Cross of his Son.[iii]

All   Let us meditate on the truth of the Cross of Christ.

Pause for reflection

Priest   The suffering of God, universally and in the Christ, is the power which overcomes creaturely self-destruction by participation and transformation.[iv]

All   Let us meditate on the truth of the Cross of Christ.

Pause for reflection

Priest   In Jesus Christ God has again and expressly claimed the whole of creation as His work, adopting it and as it were taking it to heart in both its positive and negative aspects.[v]

All   Let us meditate on the truth of the Cross of Christ.

Pause for reflection

93

Priest   God does not desire to be glorified without his liberated creation.[vi]

All   Let us meditate on the truth of the Cross of Christ.

Pause for reflection

Priest   Only the suffering God can help.[vii]

All   Let us meditate on the truth of the Cross of Christ.

Pause for reflection

Priest   Holy Father
help us
to discern
the mystery
of the Cross
of your Son
Jesus Christ;

to grasp the truth
that you identify
with the weak,
the vulnerable
and the innocent;

that your face
is seen
in all the faces
of suffering
in our world;

that no life
of any creature
is futile
or without hope;

that all pain
shall be
transfigured
by your love;

and to see the
Cross as the living
sign of your presence
with all creatures
who suffer and die.
Amen.

First   Many people were shocked when they saw him;
Reading   he was so disfigured that he hardly looked human.
He had no dignity or beauty
to make us take notice of him.
There was nothing attractive about him,
nothing that would draw us to him.
We despised him and rejected him;
he endured suffering and pain.
No one would even look at him –
we ignored him as if he were nothing.
He was treated harshly, but endured it humbly;
he never said a word.
Like a lamb about to be slaughtered,
like a sheep about to be sheared,
he never said a word.
He was arrested and sentenced and led off to die,
and no one cared about his fate
(Isa. 52.14, 53.2b–3, 7–8a, TEV)

There follows a period of silence

Priest   Lamb of God
you have become
the defenceless

95

the despised and the outcast;
help us to see
your suffering in
all the innocents
subject to our power.
Amen.

Second   Christ was as defenceless, and as innocent,
Reading as a lamb is. Since, then, scripture compares Him
to this inoffensive and unprotected animal, we
may without presumption or irreverence take this
image as a means of conveying to our minds
those feelings which our Lord's suffering should
excite within us. I mean, consider how very
horrible it is to read accounts which sometimes
meet us of cruelties exercised on brute animals ...
What was this but the very cruelty inflicted on
our Lord?

Now what is it that moves our very hearts, and
sickens us so much as cruelty shown to brutes? I
suppose this first, that they have done no harm;
next, that they have no power of resistance; it is
the cowardice and tyranny of which they are the
victims that makes their suffering so especially
touching... there is something so dreadful, so
satanic in tormenting those who have never
harmed us, and who cannot defend themselves,
who are utterly in our power, who have weapons
neither of offence or defence, that none but very
hardened persons can endure the thought of it.
Think then, my brethren, of your feelings at
cruelty practised on brute animals, and you will
gain one sort of feeling which the history of
Christ's Cross and Passion ought to excite within
you.[viii]

A Vigil for All Suffering Creatures

There follows a period of silence

All   Spirit of the living
and crucified Christ
come to us and help
us to repent
of the callousness,
indifference and cruelty
of our lives;

Pause for reflection

All   our wanton, neglectful
treatment of other creatures;

Pause for reflection

All   our lack of courage
in speaking up
for the defenceless;

Pause for reflection

All   the timidity of
our wills, and
the shallowness of
our hearts;

Pause for reflection

All   and our failure to see
the wounded Christ
in all creaturely
suffering.

Priest   Lord God
Father of the Crucified

receive our prayer
for repentance and
forgive us;
may your liberating Spirit
be upon us and
make us the voice
of the voiceless.
Amen.

Priest   To stand with Christ

All   is to stand against evil.

Priest   We cannot stand with Christ

All   and sit on the sidelines.

Priest   To stand with Christ

All   is to take sides:

Priest   To take sides against the routinized, institutionalized abuse of millions of animals in laboratories.

To take sides against the systems of intensive farming: veal crates, hen batteries, sow stalls.

To take sides against wanton killing, hunting for sport, the slaughter of seals, the barbarity of whaling.

All   We oppose the evil of inflicting suffering on innocent creatures.

Priest   We commit ourselves to Christ's work of bringing healing and redemption to the animal world.

A Vigil for All Suffering Creatures

Third Reading   I could not but feel with a sympathy full of regret all the pain that I saw around me, not only that of [human beings], but that of the whole creation. From this community of suffering, I have never tried to withdraw myself. It seemed to me a matter of course that we should all take our share of the burden of suffering which lies upon the world.[ix]

There follows a period of silence

Priest   Holy Father
the message of the Cross
of your Son
is sheer folly
to those on the way
to destruction
but to us it is
your very power;

to shame the wise
you have chosen
what the world
calls folly,
and to shame the strong
you have chosen
what the world
calls weakness;

you have chosen things
without rank
or standing
in the world,
mere nothings
to overthrow
the existing order.
(I Cor. 1. 18, 27–28, REB)

99

Give us grace
to keep this truth
and to show it
in our lives;

and may the blessing
of the same God
whose power is
shown in weakness
be upon us
now, this day,
and for ever.
Amen.

---

i   John Austin Baker
ii   Eberhard Jüngel
iii   Jürgen Moltmann
iv   Paul Tillich
v   Karl Barth
vi   Jürgen Moltmann
vii   Dietrich Bonhoeffer
viii John Henry Newman
ix   Albert Schweitzer

8

Forms for the Blessing of Animals

Of the many possible definitions, Karl Barth's interpretation of 'blessing' as the 'authorization to be' is the most appropriate here. Barth offers this interpretation in relation to the great primordial blessings uttered by God in the first story of creation (Gen. 1.22, 28): 'A thing is blessed when it is authorized and empowered, with a definite promise of success, for one particular action as distinct from another ...'.[1] Thus the act of blessing is inseparable from the divine grant of land, living space, indeed life itself. The subversive implications of this definition should not go unnoticed. God authorizes the animals' own autonomous being and freedom – to be as they are as God intended them. By blessing animals, therefore, we align ourselves with God's own allowance of freedom to other creatures, even – dare I say it – their own right to be themselves and to be free.

If this line of interpretation is correct, there is something fitting about blessing animals especially those confined, made captive, or restrained by human exploitation. To 'bless' in this context is to recognize God's own prior will in relation to these other creatures and to place ourselves on the right side in relation to them. To bless is to acknowledge God's own gift of life and liberty to the animal world. Thankfully there is a long tradition of blessing animals within the Christian tradition, though frequently the practice has seldom been understood as more than a general statement of divine benevolence.

Although animal blessings are not uncommon, there are

sections of the church where they are still resisted or viewed with suspicion. It is difficult to see the theological grounds for this resistance. Indeed, animals have a claim infinitely superior to many other current recipients. Only a very muddled church practice can entertain blessings for battle-ships or automobiles, not to mention whaling ships, but cavil about blessing animals who are God's own creatures and whose Spirit gifts them the 'breath of life' (Gen. 1.30).

For companion animals

> Fellow creature,
> friend and companion;
> may God
> your Creator and preserver,
> bless, defend, and keep you
> this day and for ever.
> Amen.

> Generous God
> whose own self-giving
> is reflected in the
> love and devotion
> of these animal companions;
> bless them
> with your Spirit,
> and make us mindful
> of the great responsibility
> we bear for
> all creatures
> dependent upon us
> for their welfare;
> help us to use
> our power over them
> for their own benefit

and never selfishly
for our own gain.
Amen.

Creator God
your mercies are over
all the earth;
bless this creature (*Name*)
and help us to delight
in all the works of your hands.
Amen.

Holy God
whose loving care
extends to
all living things;
bless and protect
this creature (*Name*)
which you have put
into our hands
and help us to
cherish *his/her* life
knowing that all life is
precious in your sight.
Amen.

Blessed be the Lord
of the earth and the heavens
who loves each living thing
and may the blessing of the Lord
be upon this creature (*Name*)
by whose providence
all life in earth and heaven
is preserved
and by whose grace
all creation shall be redeemed.
Amen.

May this creature
be a blessing to me
and me to *him/her*
in the name of the One
who blesses all those
whose life is a blessing
to others.
Amen.

For abused and suffering animals

Creator God
we pray in this place
for creatures who are abused
and who suffer terribly
at human hands:
be with them and bless them,
strengthen and comfort them
and grant them with us
a share in your eternal kingdom.
Amen.

Creator of all
as you blessed
the living creatures
at the beginning
of the world,
we pray that
you will now bless,
preserve and heal
these suffering creatures
and protect them from
all cruelty:
we ask this prayer
through the One

who showed mercy
and whose life
was a blessing
to others.
Amen.

Lord God
you have made
all creatures free
but we have imprisoned them:
in zoos for our entertainment,
in laboratories for our curiosity,
and in factory farms for our food;
But you God
are the God of liberation:
no cry of pain is unheard in heaven
and no injustice escapes your judgment;
we pray for your blessing
on all these innocent creatures
who suffer for our sake
but who are never forgotten
in your sight.
Amen.

Lord God
your creatures
suffer everywhere
at the hands of human beings
afflicted with littleness of heart;
may your blessing be upon them,
and may your Spirit
also enlarge the hearts
of their persecutors
that they may repent of their evil
and embrace the way of peace.
Amen.

For animals that are dying

> Creator God
> in whose sight
> all life is holy
> and before whom
> all the creatures
> of the earth
> are remembered;
> bless this creature (*Name*)
> with your Holy Spirit
> and grant *him/her* with us
> a share in
> your eternal kingdom.
> Amen.
>
> Dear God
> you have enlivened
> all the creatures
> of the earth
> with your Spirit;
> nothing dies
> but is remembered by you
> and nothing lives
> without your grace;
> bless this innocent creature (*Name*)
> and by your same Spirit
> grant *him/her* and all your creatures
> eternal life in your presence.
> Amen.

For those who care for animals

> Blessed before you, O God
> are those who struggle for

peace and justice
not only for human beings
but for all creatures;
strengthen their endeavours
by the power of your Holy Spirit,
and may the blessing of God Almighty,
Father, Son and Holy Spirit
be upon them.
Amen.

Blessing God
who gives strength
to those who struggle
and to those who endure;
bless us with a compassionate heart
that feels with you the
injustice of the world,
and help us to strive
towards that peaceable kingdom
in which all your creatures
shall be free from pain
and live with you
for all eternity.
Amen.

9

A Liturgy for Animal Burial

There are at least two good reasons why we should mark the death of animals. The first is theological. The God who creates is also the God who redeems – not just human beings but the entire creation. This is not some new post-modern notion; it is the biblical and – for most of the history of the church – the established view. Indeed the 1998 Lambeth Conference of Anglican bishops reaffirms historic teaching without dissent: 'the redemptive purpose of God in Jesus Christ extends to the whole of creation' (1.8 Creation (iii)). Animal burial services are an appropriate way of registering the redemptive love of God; they provide an opportunity to give thanks, and to commend the life of the sentient individual concerned into the hands of God.

Indeed within a biblically-informed perspective, there is a stronger case for the inclusion of non-human (as well as human) sentients within the sphere of redemption than any other creature. The reason is obvious. In the case of animals, they can suffer and can therefore clearly be harmed. Animals, we can properly suppose, have something to be redeemed from, *namely the 'bondage to decay' and the groans and sighs to which they are currently subject (Rom. 8.18–24). John Wesley's statement of the future recompense owing to suffering animals cannot be bettered: '... they shall enjoy happiness suited to their state, without alloy, without interruption, and without end'.[1]*

Neither can Wesley be gainsaid when he asks, 'But what end does it answer to dwell upon this subject which we so imperfectly understand [the future life of animals]?' and answers: 'It may soften our hearts towards the meaner creatures, knowing that the Lord cares for them', and again: 'It may enlarge our hearts towards these poor creatures, to reflect that, as vile as they appear in our eyes, not one of them is forgotten in the sight of our Father which is in heaven.'[2]

The second reason is pastoral. Anyone who has shared his or her life with a companion animal will know the terrible sense of loss occasioned by its death. Such is the reality of the human-animal bond that the experience of bereavement can be as deep, sometimes even deeper, than the loss of another human subject.[3] Christian theology has simply failed to recognize both the spiritual significance of animal-human companionship and the sense of spiritual desolation bequeathed by its loss. Hence churches in practice have very little to offer those in the throes of bereavement, indeed frequently express hostility or ridicule when faced with it. To those suffering such bereavement it is as inconceivable that the body of their departed companion should be thrown out as garbage without a prayer as it would be in the case of the dead body of any human companion.

Liturgical practice needs to make up for theological insensitivity in this area as a matter of urgency. What follows is a basic order centred on the promise of redemption in Christ for all creation with alternative prayers for dedication and commital. As new liturgical practice develops in this area (as I am sure it will), we shall be astonished that it took us so long a time to see that the Gospel message of hope has relevance to all creatures – both to those who have died and those who grieve for them.

Priest   I saw a new heaven and a new earth: for the first heaven and the first earth were passed away. And he shall wipe away all tears from their eyes; and there shall be no more death, neither sorrow, nor

crying, neither shall there be any more pain: for the former things are passed away. And he that sat upon the throne said, Behold I make all things new. I am Alpha and Omega, the beginning and the end.
(*Rev. 21.1, 4–5a, 6, RSV*)

Christ is the first and the last,
the Alpha and the Omega;

All   who reconciles and redeems
every form of created life.

Priest   Christ is the first and the last,
the Alpha and the Omega;

All   the source and destiny
of all living things.

Priest   Christ is the first and the last,
the Alpha and the Omega;

All   who bears the wounds of
all suffering creatures.

Priest   Christ is the first and the last,
the Alpha and the Omega;

All   who transforms all
suffering into joy.

Priest   St John saw the
new heaven and earth;
a place without pain
where there will be
no more sorrow or crying.

A Liturgy for Animal Burial

St Paul wrote that the
sufferings of the present time
are not worth comparing
with the joy that we find
after death in Christ.

This promise of joy
after our present sufferings
is God's gift to all creatures.

We do not mourn, therefore,
without hope, and especially
without thanksgiving.

For the same God who creates
is the same God who reconciles
and redeems all creation.

All   Christ is the first and the last
the Alpha and the Omega;
the Saviour of the Universe:
in Christ shall all be made alive.

*One or more of the following prayers of dedication and
commital may be said*

A

Priest   It is God's love that speaks to me
in the birds and streams ...[i]

Holy Creator
give us eyes to see
and ears to hear
how every living thing
speaks to us of your love.

Animal Rites

Let us be awestruck
at your creation
and daily sing your praises.

Enable us to rejoice
that we are alive
among so many miracles
of your grace.

Especially, we pray,
create within us
a spirit of gratitude
for the life of (*Name*)
who lived among us
and gave us freely of *his/her* love.

Receive this life
which we commit into your hands
and in a world of ingratitude
receive also from us
our heartful prayer
of thanksgiving.

Even in our sorrow
we have cause for joy
for we know that
this creature
who died on earth
shall live again in heaven

and your power which sets
the moon and the stars
shall unite us again
with the face of (*Name*)
and all the other faces
of your love
in another world
according to your grace.

A Liturgy for Animal Burial

For in that place
we shall see and we shall know
and most of all we shall love.

Most loving God
mysterious beyond all worlds
your indestructible love
embraces every living thing.
Amen.

B

Priest   Pilgrim God
who journeys with us
through the joys and shadows
of this world

be with us
in our sorrow
and feel our pain;

help us to accept
the mystery of death
without bitterness
but with hope.

Among the shadows
of this world,
amid the turmoil of life
and the fear of death

you stand alongside us,
always blessing, always giving,
arms always outstretched.

For this we know:
every living thing is yours
and returns to you.

As we ponder this mystery
we give you thanks
for the life of (*Name*)
and we now commit *him/her*
into your loving hands.

Gentle God:
fragile is your world,
delicate are your creatures,
and costly is your love
which bears and redeems us all.
Amen.

C

Priest   Holy Father
your Son Jesus Christ
taught us that not one sparrow
is forgotten in your sight;

we ask you now to remember
our friend and companion (*Name*)
whose life was blessed
by the gift of your Spirit
and whose life among us
on earth has ended.

Receive now we pray the
life of (*Name*)
which we commit into your hands.

Take pity, dear Lord, on this innocent creature
whose life, like ours, was burdened with
suffering and pain, and grant us with *him/her*
a share in your eternal kingdom.

Eternal Father, we know that nothing
can finally separate us from those we love

and that in another place and another time
we shall be reunited with all those earthly faces
whom we have loved and for whom we now
mourn.

We ask these prayers
through Jesus Christ
your Son, our Lord.
Amen.

D

Priest   Creator of all, everything that has breath
praises you both in this world and in the next:

heaven is full of the sounds of creaturely voices
a great cacophany of praise and thanksgiving.

Day and night your creatures praise you;
without ceasing, and with joy.

We now commit the life of this our friend
(*Name*)
to eternal fellowship with you.

May *his/her* praises be heard in your presence
where *he/she* shall be free from suffering and
pain.

Creator, hear our prayer
and let our praise
unite with those in heaven
into one long song
of eternal thanksgiving.
Amen.

E

Priest   Loving Creator
source of all life
have pity on this creature
whose life was marked by suffering and pain.

Receive this life into your presence
and grant (*Name*) that joy and happiness
he/she failed to find on earth.

Fill our own hearts with pity
for all those creatures
which suffer and grant us
time to repent for
the evil we have caused them.

We ask these prayers
through Jesus Christ
who came to bring life
to the world
and freedom from death
for all God's creatures.
Amen.

F

Priest   Living Christ
Saviour of the Universe;

Logos through whom
all things come to be;

whose Cross is the
suffering of all creatures:

A Liturgy for Animal Burial

take now and transform
the life of this poor creature (*Name*)

whose death is the common bondage
of us all;

free this creature
and all your creatures,

from the powers of death
to life everlasting.
Amen.

G

Priest   Holy Father
we have seen
the face of your
crucified Son
in the faces
of your suffering creatures;

we know that the Cross
of your Son
stretches across
the whole world;

in every cry of pain
in every broken body
your Son is with us;

receive now the life
of this fellow victim (*Name*)

that as you have been
with *him/her* in life
you may also restore *him/her*
in death;

through Jesus Christ
who alone is our hope
on earth and in heaven
our sure reward.
Amen.

Concluding prayer

All   O God, before whom
generations rise and fall
and countless creatures live and die:
liberate us from earthly despair
and help us to see your transforming power
even in what appears most devastating to us.

Most especially we pray for the grace
to live and believe your Gospel so that
one day all creation shall be set free
and your kingdom established
on earth as in heaven;

through Jesus Christ
the first and the last,
the Alpha and the Omega
whose triumph over death
is our hope of eternal life.
Amen.

---

i Thomas Merton

10

Memorial Prayers for Animals

The function of memorials is to help us remember. In almost all cities and towns we see monuments and memorials to human beings who have died (most usually in war) or who have lived especially courageous or selfless lives. There are few memorials, however, to mark the many millions of animals who have been killed or abused in order to make the lives of human beings easier or more comfortable.

One such memorial is the now re-established brown dog statue in Battersea Park in remembrance of the dog who was vivisected at University College, London.[1] Another is the memorial stone at the University of Guelph in Canada 'in recognition of the animals used' in research and teaching. The stone memorial was erected in 1993 following the first university memorial service for laboratory animals who had died in the course of the university's research.[2]

It is important that we should remember that we frequently live at the expense of other creatures and the nature of our debt to the animal world. We shall not change the world for animals or our own exploitative practices if we do not remember, acknowledge, and attend to the harm that is done to them. This requires an effort of the will: a deliberate act of bringing into our consciousness what our current lifestyles cost other sentient creatures. Remembering is part of the quest for spiritual wholeness.

Sadly, churches which could have helped lead the way in providing such rituals have largely scorned them. Now is the time for a fundamental rethink. The increased ethical sensitivity to animals which is emerging among us needs liturgical markers and rituals to help us integrate the recognition of our daily violence to other species into our spiritual consciousness of the world. What follows are three forms of memorial prayers. The first is generally for animals who have suffered and died at human hands, the second is specifically for the unveiling of a memorial stone or plaque, and the third is for use outside a place or institution where animals have died.

It may be thought that the act of remembering is a small response to the daily crucifixion that animals have had to undergo at our hands. And in purely human terms, it surely is. But from a Christian perspective re-membering is not just the commemoration of the past but rather the bringing of the past into the present in such a way that the present is decisively transformed. Remembrance is an inseparable part of the process of spiritual transformation.

Prayers for animals who have suffered and died

Priest So I returned and considered all the oppressions
    that are done under the sun; and behold the tears
    of such as were oppressed, and they had no
    comforter ... Wherefore I praised the dead which
    are already dead more than the living which are
    yet alive. *(Eccles. 4.1–2)*

There follows a period of silence

Priest Holy God
    our oppression of the
    animal world
    is relentless and unremitting;

    there is hardly a species left
    on earth which has not been
    subject to our misuse of power.

All   We have become vain exploiters
of your good earth;
taking and using other
creatures with no thought
for you their Creator.

Priest   O God, you have given us
temporary lordship
of your creation;
to care in your name for
all the creatures of the earth;

All   but looking at our wickedness
and our violence on the face
of the earth
you repented of our creation

Priest   and your fateful words have
reverberated around
the earth:
' I am sorry that
I have made them'. *(Gen. 6.6)*

All   Yet you still forgave us
and established a covenant with us
and all living creatures;

as we remember your covenant
we bring to mind
our continuing violence
to the earth and our
neglect of our
fellow creatures.

Priest   We pray, Holy God,
that you will renew

us with your Spirit
and help us
to remember
and to repent

for you have 'made your
wonderful works to be remembered;
the Lord is gracious and full
of compassion'.
(Ps. 111.4)

All Help us to
turn to the
animal world
and to see again
the violence
we have wrought on the face
of the earth

for 'who teaches us
more than the creatures
of the earth
and makes us wiser
than the birds of heaven?'
(Job 35.11)

Priest Especially we remember:

those animals
who have died
for food, for entertainment,
for sport, and for science
in laboratories, abbatoirs,
zoos and factory farms;

unlike us
they were innocent
of evil;

they have not sacrificed
their lives,
we have stolen them;

they were sentient creatures
enjoyed by God

but we treated them
as resources here for us;

we have lived our lives
at the expense of their death.

All   As we remember them
help us to repent.

Priest   As you, O God,
repented of our creation
and yet made anew
through the establishment
of your covenant
with all creatures

enable us to be
so full of remorse
for our oppression
of the animal world
that we may
bring good out of our evil

and learn to live
without violence;

All   always remembering
that nothing lives
without your blessing
and nothing dies
without your care.

Priest As we remember and repent,
we pray that
you, Holy God,
source of all life,
will remember us
when we also
return to dust.

For that which befalls
humanity also befalls
the animals ... as one dies
so does the other ...
yes, they all have one
breath and humans have no
pre-eminence over the animals.
All go unto one place; all are
of the dust, and all turn
to dust again.
(Eccles. 3. 19–20)

Prayers for the unveiling of a memorial stone or plaque
in memory of animals that have died

Priest Heavenly Father
your love and justice
encompasses all creation;
there is no injustice
which will not be righted
and no wrong left unknown.

For you know
the secrets of our hearts
and our misdeeds
are ever before you;

no cry of pain
no untimely death
no cruel thought or deed
is unremembered in your sight.

O God who remembers all creation,
every little creature,
and every work of evil:
help us to remember
those animals
who have suffered
and died for us;

help us to turn towards
the evil we have done
and remember it;
and in remembering
be filled with shame for
the works of our hands.

Remembering God
you are also a
compassionate God
who forgives all
those who truly
remember and repent
of the ways of
sinfulness.

Most Holy God
bless this *stone/plaque*
which we dedicate to you
in memory of all those
fellow creatures who have
suffered and died
in this place;

may it be for us
a sign of what
we have done
and, inspired by your grace,
what we may yet do
to alleviate the harm
we inflict on the
animal world.

There follows a period of silence

Priest	You hear the cries of all your creatures
All	Your judgment is upon us, O Lord.
Priest	You know our unloving and uncaring hearts
All	Your judgment is upon us, O Lord.
Priest	You know our secret ways of cruelty
All	Your judgment is upon us, O Lord.
Priest	Fill us with shame and remorse
All	Your judgment is upon us, O Lord.
Priest	Accept this sign of our repentance
All	Your judgment is upon us, O Lord.
Priest	Turn us from darkness to light
All	Your judgment is upon us, O Lord.

Priest   Merciful God
have mercy even on ourselves:
deliver us from our
narrowness of vision
and the moral parochialism
of our lives;

as we remember the
lives of other creatures
who have died
enlarge within us
a sense of your mercies
over all your works
and rekindle within us
a new spirit of fraternity
so that we who have
walked in the ways of violence
may become agents of
your peace.

All   Leave us not, O God;

Priest   remember us and all creatures
as we come into your kingdom.
Amen.

Prayers outside a place or institution where animals have
suffered and died

All   Your mercy, O God,
reaches unto the heavens;
and your faithfulness
unto the clouds.

Your righteousness stands
like the strong mountains,

your judgments are like
the great deep:

O Lord, you save
both humans and animals.
(Ps. 36.5–6)

Priest   Holy God
we do not know
why you allow the
weak and the innocent
to suffer at our hands;

millions of animals
suffer every year
for our vanity,
curiosity and greed.

All   We who have been given
power to do good
have turned
our backs on you;
used our power
for our own ends
and accomplished evil.

Priest   Specifically, in this place
hundreds and thousands
of creatures have died:
without our shame or sorrow;

we have not heard their cries,
we have cared little for their lives,
and their deaths have gone unmourned.

There follows a period of silence

All   God of justice
fill us with
righteous anger
at the complacency
and callousness
of our lives.

Priest   God of mercy
drive from us
our hardness of heart
and renew your Spirit
of pity within us.

All   God of salvation
who redeems every creature
in your Son
and whose triumph over death
is the hope of all creation;

we remember before you
these creatures
who have died
in this place
at our hands
and we plead
for your mercy.

Priest   We cannot fathom
your justice
nor understand its bounds;
but we know
that your love
is supremely revealed
in the suffering of
the weak and vulnerable;

create in us contrite
and loving hearts;

and by the same Spirit
such a sense of penitence
that in our remembrance
of past evil

we may have grace to live
in the present

and to honour all
those fellow-creatures
who are the unacknowledged
faces of your crucified Son
in our world.

All The whole creation
was altered by your Passion;
for all things suffered
with you,
knowing, O Lord,
that you hold all things
in unity.[i]

Priest God of the universe
without boundaries
of race, creed, colour or species
in whose sight every life is precious;
send now your Spirit upon us
and liberate us
from that littleness
of mind, heart and soul
so that we may perceive
the kinship of all creatures
and work towards that goal
in which all things
will be united in Christ.
Amen.

---

i From the Byzantine Rite in *Lenten Triodion*

Appendix 1

Additional Prayers and Readings

1 You alone are unutterable,
   from the time you created all things
      that can be spoken of.
   You alone are unknowable,
   from the time you created all things
      that can be known.
   All things cry out about you;
   those which speak,
      and those which cannot speak.
   All things honour you;
   those which think,
      and those which cannot think.
   For there is one longing, one groaning,
      that all things have for you ...

   All things pray to you that comprehend
      your plan
   and offer you a silent hymn.
   In you, the One, all things abide,
   and all things endlessly run to you
   who are the end of all.

   St Gregory Nazianzen

2 Love all God's creation, the whole of it and every grain of
   sand. Love every leaf, every ray of God's light! Love the
   animals, love the plants, love everything. If you love everything, you will perceive the divine mystery in things. And

once you have perceived it, you will begin to comprehend it ceaselessly, more and more every day. And you will at last come to love the whole world with an abiding, universal love. Love the animals: God has given them the rudiments of thought and untroubled joy. Do not, therefore, trouble [them], do not torture them, do no deprive them of their joy, do not go against God's intent.

Fyodor Mikhail Dostoyevsky

3 How the beasts groan!
    The herds of cattle are perplexed
because there is no pasture for them;
    even the flocks of sheep are dismayed.
'Fear not, O land;
    be glad and rejoice,
    for the Lord has done great things!
Fear not, you beasts of the field,
    for the pastures of the wilderness are green;
the tree bears its fruit,
    the fig tree and the vine give their full yield.'

Joel 1.18, 2.21–22

4 [I was shown] something small, no bigger than a hazel-nut, lying in the palm of my hand, and I perceived that it was as round as any ball. I looked at this and thought: What can this be? And I was given this general answer: It is everything which is made. I was amazed that it could last, for I thought that it was so little that it could suddenly fall into nothing. And I was answered in my understanding: It lasts and always will, because God loves it; and thus everything has being through the love of God. In this little thing I saw three properties. The first is that God made it, the second is that [God] loves it, the third is that God preserves it. But what is

that to me? It is that God is the Creator and the lover and the protector.

   Julian of Norwich

5 If I were to speak to the Emperor, I would, supplicating and persuading him, tell him for the love of God and me to make a special law that no [person] should take or kill sister larks, nor do them any harm. Likewise that all the Podestas of the towns, and the lords of castles and villages, should be bound every year on Christmas day to compel [people] to throw wheat and other grains outside the cities and castles, that our sister larks may have something to eat, and also the other birds, on a day of such solemnity. And that for the reverence of the Son of God, who rested on that night with the Most Blessed Virgin Mary between an ox and an ass in the manger, whoever shall have an ox and an ass shall be bound to provide for them on that night the best of good fodder. Likewise on that day, all poor [people] should be satisfied by the rich with good food.

   St Francis of Assisi

6 St Francis is before us also as an example of unalterable meekness and sincere love with regard to irrational beings who make up part of creation. In him re-echoes that harmony that is illustrated with striking words in the first pages of the Bible: 'God placed man in the garden of Eden to cultivate it and care for it' (Genesis 2.15), and he 'brought the animals to man to see what he would name them' (Genesis 2.19). In St Francis we glimpse almost an anticipation of that peace proposed by Sacred Scripture, when 'the wolf shall dwell with the lamb, and the leopard shall lie down with the kid, and the calf and the lion shall graze together, and a child shall lead them' (Isaiah 11.16). He looked upon creation with the eyes of one

who could recognize in it the marvellous work of the hand of God. His voice, his glance, his solicitous care, not only towards [human beings], but also towards animals and nature in general, are a faithful echo of the love with which God in the beginning ... had brought them into existence ...

We too are called to a similar attitude. Created in the image of God, we must make [God] present among creatures 'as intelligent and noble masters and guardians of nature and not as heedless exploiters and destroyers' (Encyclical Letter, *Redemptor Hominis*, 15).

Pope John Paul II

7 If you have heard the singing of the birds or the running of the stream, or the voices of children as you came to church, then reflect it was Christ who caused you to hear them. He fills the earth and the air with all medodies, and he gives [us] the power of taking them in.

F. D. Maurice

8 [Our] treatment of animals is a sadly neglected province in the field of Christian ethics, and the detailed record of Christendom in regard to it would repay a much fuller investigation than has yet been given to it ... The gross brutality to which the habits of sport and even of flesh-eating have inured most Christian consciences obviously yields but slowly before the insistent reproaches of those nobler and tenderer feelings which the Spirit of God has implanted within us and which the Christian discipline serves to enhance and develop.

C. J. Cadoux

9 The Spirit immediately drove him out into the wilderness. And he was in the wilderness forty days, tempted by Satan;

and he was with the wild beasts; and the angels ministered to
him.

Mark 1. 12–13

10 Christ of His gentleness
Thirsting and hungering
Walked in the wilderness;
Soft words of grace He spoke
Unto lost desert-folk
That listened wondering.
He heard the bitterns call
From the ruined palace wall,
Answered them brotherly;
He held communion
With the she-pelican
Of lonely piety.
Basilisk, cockatrice,
Flocked to His homilies,
With mail of dread device,
With monstrous barbed slings,
With eager dragon-eyes;
Great rats on leather wings,
And poor blind broken things,
Foul in their miseries.
And ever with Him went,
Of all His wanderings
Comrade, with ragged coat,
Gaunt ribs – poor innocent –
Bleeding foot, burning throat,
The guileless old scapegoat;
For forty nights and days
Followed in Jesus' ways,
Sure guard behind Him kept,
Tears like a lover wept.

Robert Graves

11 When I was young I often heard quoted a piece of Christian philosophy which was taken as self-evidently true. It was the proposition that animals have no rights. This, of course, is true only in one sense. They are not human persons and therefore they have no rights, so to speak, in their own right. But they have very positive rights because they are God's creatures. If we have to speak with absolute accuracy we must say that God has the right to have all ... creatures treated with proper respect.

Nobody should therefore carelessly repeat the old saying that animals have no rights. This could easily lead to wanton cruelty. I speak of wanton cruelty because only the perverted are guilty of deliberate cruelty to animals or, indeed, to children. The difficulty is that many people do not realize the extent to which cruelty is practised as a matter of business ... It was once pointed out to me that the catechism had no question about cruelty to animals. This was true, but in giving lessons on Christian doctrine teachers now include the subject of cruelty to animals. The best and most experienced teachers do not, of course, talk of cruelty to animals. They talk of kindness to animals. Christians have a duty not only to refrain from doing harm but also to do positive good.

Cardinal Heenan

12 I cannot think it extravagant to imagine, that [human]kind are no less, in proportion, accountable for the ill use of their dominion over creatures of the lower rank of beings, than for the exercise of tyranny over their own species.

Alexander Pope

13 And the Lord said, 'You pity the plant, for which you did not labour, nor did you make it grow, which came into being in a night, and perished in a night. And should not I pity

Nineveh, that great city, in which there are more than a hundred and twenty thousand persons who do not know their right hand from their left, and also much cattle?'

Jonah 4. 10–11

14 We praise you for the creation of the world and all the living creatures in the earth, sky and sea.
We are thankful, O God.

For the gentle eyes of the deer, the friendship of dogs, the purr of cats, the strength of bears, the beauty of a hippo, the humour of chimps, the intelligence of gorillas, the grace of dolphins, and the magnificence of whales. Help us to keep them safe.
We are thankful, O God.

For the bond between all living creatures created by the same author, and for the memory of our kinship to the animal world kindled each time a rainbow appears.
We are thankful, O God.

Keep us mindful of the vision of the peaceable kingdom in which all living creatures dwell in harmony.
This we pray, O God.

Give us a voice to speak in protest when any of your beloved creatures are treated cruelly. Help us to be advocates for those innocents who cannot speak for themselves.
Give us speech, O God.

Give us ears to hear the cries of those creatures tortured in the name of science, skinned in the name of fashion, and neglected in the name of economy.
Let us hear their cries, O God.

Give us eyes to see our responsibilities, not just to the human community, but to the community of all living creatures. Let us be mindful of the rabbinic injunction that, 'The way a person treats an animal is an index to their soul.'
Help us to see, O God.

In this world so full of violence and unkindness, let us act in a gentle way towards all your creatures. A simple stroke on a dog's head, a scratch on a cat's chin, food for birds in winter and hunting with cameras only.
Help us to be gentle, O God.

Help us to lessen the suffering of your creatures, O God. Hasten the coming of your kingdom when the sun will shine on all your creation living in peace and love.

We pray this, O Lord. Help us to be kind and gentle like our Lord Jesus. And may we remember St Francis' love of animals whenever we see one of your creatures hurt, suffering, and in need of help.

Robert A. Everett

15 'For the expectation of the creature waiteth for the revelation of the sons of God ... Because the creature also itself shall be delivered from the servitude of corruption into the liberty of the children of God' (Rom. 8.19–21).

Upon our hope, therefore, depends the liberty of the whole universe. Because our hope is the pledge of a new heaven and a new earth, in which all things will be what they were meant to be. They will rise, together with us, in Christ. The beasts and trees will one day share with us a new creation and we will see them as God sees them and know that they are very good.

Thomas Merton

16 And other eyes than ours
    Were made to look on flowers,
    Eyes of small birds and insects small:
    The deep sun-blushing rose
    Round which the prickles close
    Opens her bosom to them all.
    The tiniest living thing
    That soars on feathered wing,
    Or crawls among the long grass out of sight
    Has just as good a right
    To its appointed portion of delight
    As any King.

    Christina Rossetti

17 [T]hink of [the Spirit's] operations, their countless number,
    their unspeakable greatness, and their boundless range,
    before creation, in the creature, in the ages to come ... There
    is indeed not one single gift which reaches creation without
    the Holy Spirit.

    St Basil the Great

18 The soundest of all foundations on which to build a true and
    effective concern for animals is humility, reverence, awe in
    face of the mystery we call LIFE. There are times when we
    have to take the lives of the more developed sentient
    creatures, either in mercy or in self-defence. But how sad it is
    when, with no justification but that of material gain, we
    violate a genuine awareness, yes, we must say of the holiness
    of life, by needless killing ... Yet saddest of all, most terrible
    of all fates surely, is to have lost that sense of the holiness of
    life altogether, to be so unaware of the true nature of the
    creatures with which we are dealing that we commit the
    blasphemy, the sacrilege of bringing thousands of lives to a

cruel and terrifying death, or making those lives a living death – and feel nothing … It is in the battery shed and the broiler house, not in the wild, that we find the true parallel to Auschwitz. Auschwitz is a purely human invention.

John Austin Baker

19 The lavishness and endlessness of natural beauty is a thing to be wondered at. Sunsets and sunrises are going on all the time, and sunlight is running through trees and blades of grass, and shining on great icebergs and caverns all through the day; a few seconds of this multitudinous riot of colour and light and beauty are noticed occasionally by a few human beings, but it is good to see how utterly irrelevant we are to these displays … It is good to realize that God has other interests besides [human beings].

Francis Hugh Maycock

20 The reason why God's servants love [God's] creatures so deeply is that they realize how deeply Christ loves them. And it is the very character of love to love what is loved by those we love.

St Catherine of Siena

21 One must remember that the Christian belief is that there is an existence after earthly life which is so glorious that it makes any earthly suffering pall in comparison; and that such eternal life is internally related to acts and sufferings of worldly life, so that they contribute to, and are essential parts of, the sort of glory which is to come. The Christian paradigm here is the resurrection body of Jesus, which is glorious beyond description, but which still bears the wounds of the cross (John 20. 27). So the sufferings of this life are not just

obliterated; they are transfigured by joy, but always remain as contributory factors to make us the sort of individual beings we are eternally.

This must be true for the whole of creation, insofar as it has sentience at all. If there is any sentient being which suffers pain, that being – whatever it is and however it is manifested – must find that pain transfigured by a greater joy. I am quite agnostic as to how this is to happen; but that it must be asserted to be true follows from the doctrine that God is love and would not therefore create any being whose sole destiny was to suffer pain.

Keith Ward

22 And for all this, nature is never spent;
　　There lives the dearest freshness deep down things ...
　　Because the Holy Ghost over the bent
　　World broods with warm breast and with ah! bright wings.

Gerard Manley Hopkins

23 Hear, O my people, and I will speak,
　　　O Israel, I will testify against you.
　　　I am God, your God.
　　I do not reprove you for your sacrifices;
　　　your burnt offerings are continually before me.
　　I will accept no bull from your house,
　　　nor he-goat from your folds.
　　For every beast of the forest is mine,
　　　the cattle on a thousand hills.
　　I know all the birds of the air,
　　　and all that moves in the field is mine.

Psalm 50. 7–11

24 [I] was early convinced in my mind that true religion consisted in an inward life, wherein the heart doth love and reverence God the Creator and learn to exercise true justice and goodness not only toward all [people] but also toward the [animal] creatures; that as the mind was moved on an inward principle to love God as an invisible, incomprehensible being, on the same principle it was moved to love [God] in all [the] manifestations in the visible world; and as by [God's] breath the flame of life was kindled in all animal and sensitive creatures, to say we love God as unseen and at the same time exercise cruelty toward the least creature moving by [God's] life, or by life derived from [God] was a contradiction in itself.

John Woolman

25 No matter that [humans] in their hundreds and thousands disfigured the land on which they swarmed, paved the ground with stones so that no green thing could grow, filled the air with the fumes of coal and gas, lopped back all the trees, and drove away every animal or bird: spring was still spring even in the town ... Plants, birds, insects and children rejoiced. But [humans], adult [humans], never ceased to cheat and harass their fellows and themselves. What [humans] considered sacred and important was not the spring morning, not the beauty of God's world given for the enjoyment of all creatures, not the beauty which inclines the heart to peace and love and concord. What [humans] considered sacred and important were their own devices for wielding power over their fellow [human beings].

Leo Tolstoy

26 We who realize that we are pilgrims and stewards recognize that our claim on the earth and its resources is not absolute:

neither as individuals nor as a generation do we have the right to appropriate for ourselves what God has given to all. We must learn and live the biblical teaching that we should relate to the land and to each other in a spirit of harmony and of sharing.

John Hart

27 Jesus sent two disciples, saying to them, 'Go into the village opposite you, and immediately you will find an ass tied, and a colt with her; untie them and bring them to me. If any one says anything to you, you shall say, "the Lord has need of them", and he will send them immediately.' This took place to fulfil what was spoken by the prophet, saying:
　　'Tell the daughter of Zion,
　　Behold, your king is coming to you,
　　humble and mounted on an ass,
　　and on a colt, the foal of an ass.'

Matthew 21.1b–5

28 Jesus on his ass entered Jerusalem to bring the sort of peace which Balaam on his ass had also brought in that very ancient story. It was not what the contemporary leaders in Jerusalem wanted any more than it was what Balak wanted ...

　　Jesus is, I think, rather like the protofigure in some African clan genealogy, born together with an animal – crocodile, buck or lion – and thus establishing a permanent totemic relationship with his half-brother, human with animal. Borne by the ass on which he will ride in mock triumph as a prince of peace, he becomes that sort of prince who can appropriately ride on an ass, and this is the sort of peace to which we aspire in the celebration of Christmas: a peace in which humanity humbly rediscovers kinship with the animal creation (remember the old myth that on Christmas night all the animals can speak in human tongues), an animal world over which it has ridden with no dialogue whatsoever till danger stands across the road. It is the ass, this dull, stupid fellow, who tells us what an unaggressive kingdom of peace must be all about. And that, perhaps, is the message of Christmas.

Adrian Hastings

29 Here I saw a great unity between Christ and us, as I understand it; for when he was in pain we were in pain, and all creatures able to suffer pain suffered with him.

Julian of Norwich

30 Backward among the dusky years
A lonesome lamp is seen arise,
Lit by a few fain pioneers
Before incredulous eyes. –
We read the legend that it lights:
'Wherefore beholds this land of historied rights
Mild creatures, despot-doomed, bewildered, plead
Their often hunger, thirst, pangs, prisonment,
In deep dumb gaze more eloquent
Than tongues of widest heed?'

What was faint-written, read in a breath
In that year – ten times ten away –
A larger louder conscience saith
More sturdily to-day. –
But still these innocents are thralls
To throbless hearts, near, far, that hear no calls
Of honour towards their too-dependent frail,
And from Columbia Cape to Ind we see
How helplessness breeds tyranny
In power above assail.

Cries still are heard in secret nooks,
Till hushed with gag or slit or thud;
And hideous dens whereon none looks
Are sprayed with needless blood.
But here, in battlings, patient, slow,
Much has been won – more, maybe, than we know –
And on we labour hopeful. 'Ailinon!'
A mighty voice falls: 'But may the good prevail!'
And 'Blessed are the merciful!'
Calls yet a mightier one.

    Thomas Hardy

31 Dear God
    protect and bless
    all beings that breathe,
    keep all evil from them,
    and let them sleep in peace.

    Albert Schweitzer

32 Shatter, my God,
    through the daring of your revelation
    the childishly timid outlook
    that can conceive of nothing greater
    or more vital in the world
    than the pitiable perfection
    of our human organism.

    Pierre Teilhard de Chardin

33 Incarnation is unique for the special group in which it happens, but it is not unique in the sense that other singular incarnations for other unique worlds are excluded. [Humanity] cannot claim that the infinite has entered the

finite to overcome its existential estrangement in [itself] alone. [Humanity] cannot claim to occupy the only possible place for incarnation ... Therefore, if there are non-human 'worlds' in which existential estrangement is not only real – as it is in the whole universe – but in which there is also a type of awareness of this estrangement, such worlds cannot be without the operation of the saving power within them.

Paul Tillich

34 [The Logos] produces a single melody ... holding the universe like a lyre, draws together the things in the air with those on earth, and those in the heaven with those in the air, and combines the whole with the parts, linking them with [its] command and will, and thus producing in beauty and harmony a single world and a single order within it ... [The Logos] extends [its] power everywhere, illuminating all things visible and invisible, containing and enclosing them in [itself], [giving] life and everything, everywhere, to each individually and to all together creating an exquisite single euphonious harmony.

St Athanasius

35 We must turn back to what we have left of the capacity for wonder; only reverence for life can deliver us from our inhumanity, and from the cataclysm of violence awaiting us at the end of our present road.

Laurens van der Post

36 The creatures of the sense world signify the invisible attributes of God, partly because God is the origin, exemplar and end of every creature, and every effect is the sign of its cause, the exemplification of its exemplar and the path to the end,

to which it leads ..... For every creature is by its nature a kind
of effigy and likeness of the eternal Wisdom.

Therefore, open your eyes, alert the ears of your spirit,
open your lips and apply your heart so that in all creatures
you may see, hear, praise, love and worship, glorify and
honour your God lest the whole world rise against you.

St Bonaventure

37 Oh yet we trust that somehow good
Will be the final goal of ill,
To pangs of nature, sins of will,
Defects of doubt, and taints of blood;

That nothing walks with aimless feet;
That not one life shall be destroy'd,
Or cast as rubbish to the void,
When God hath made the pile complete;

That not a worm is cloven in vain;
That not a moth with vain desire
Is shrivell'd in a fruitless fire,
Or but subserves another's gain.

Behold, we know not anything;
I can but trust that good shall fall
At last – far off – at last to all,
And every winter change to spring.

Alfred, Lord Tennyson

38 i thank You God for most this amazing
day: for the leaping greenly spirits of trees
and a blue true dream of sky; and for everything
which is natural which is infinite which is yes

E. E. Cummings

39 In the past theology has often been slow to respond to new
    points of insight and sensitivity – though later its own vision
    and its own heart have been enlarged by them: to sensitivity,
    for instance, about the iniquity of slavery and the rights of
    coloured people. Perhaps the theology of our own age will be
    convicted of myopia if it does not spend serious reflection
    upon that new kind of reverence for nature which is
    appearing among us. The present seems an opportune time
    for reflection. For the wholly anthropocentric theology of the
    last 15 or 20 years has clearly run out of inspiration and is
    degenerating towards triviality.

    W. H. Vanstone

40 And I have felt
    A presence that disturbs me with the joy
    Of elevated thoughts ...
    A motion and a spirit, that impels
    All thinking things, all objects of all thought,
    And rolls through all things. Therefore am I still
    A lover of the meadows and the woods,
    And mountains; and of all that we behold
    From this green earth ...

    William Wordsworth

41 The whole [animal] creation will then, undoubtedly, be
    restored ... Thus, in that day, all the vanity to which they
    are now helplessly subject, will be abolished; they will suffer
    no more, either from within or without; the days of their
    groaning are ended. At the same time, there can be no
    reasonable doubt, but all the horridness of their appearance,
    and all the deformities of their aspect, will vanish away, and
    be changed for their primeval beauty. And with their beauty,

their happiness will return; to which there can be no obstruction ... In the new earth, as well as the new heavens, there will be nothing to give pain, but everything that the wisdom and goodness of God can create to give happiness. As a recompense for what they once suffered, while under the 'bondage of corruption', when God has 'renewed the face of the earth', and their corruptible body has put on incorruption, they shall enjoy happiness suited to their state, without alloy, without interruption, and without end.

John Wesley

42 To see a world in a grain of sand
And a heaven in a wild flower,
Hold infinity in the palm of your hand
And eternity in an hour.

A robin redbreast in a cage
Puts all Heaven in a rage.
A dove-house filled with doves and pigeons
Shudders Hell through all its regions.
A dog starved at his master's gate
Predicts the ruin of the state.
A horse misused upon the road
Calls to Heaven for human blood.
Each outcry of the hunted hare
A fibre from the brain does tear.
A skylark wounded in the wing,
A cherubim does cease to sing.
The gamecock clipped and armed for flight
Does the rising sun affright.
Every wolf's and lion's howl
Raises from Hell a human soul.
The wild deer wandering here and there
Keeps the human soul from care...

Kill not the moth nor butterfly,
For the Last Judgment draweth nigh.

   William Blake

43   Glorious Lord Christ: the divine influence secretly diffused
     and active in the depths of matter, and the dazzling centre
     where all the innumerable fibres of the manifold meet; power
     as implacable as the world and as warm as life; you whose
     forehead is of the whiteness of snow, whose eyes are of fire,
     and whose feet are brighter than molten gold; you whose
     hands imprison the stars; you who are the first and the last,
     the living, the dead and the risen again; you who gather into
     your exuberant unity every beauty, every affinity, every
     energy, every mode of existence; it is to you to whom my
     being cries out with a desire as vast as the universe, 'In truth
     you are my Lord and my God.'

        Pierre Teilhard de Chardin

44   [I] believe that where the love of God is verily perfected and
     the true spirit of government watchfully attended to, a
     tenderness toward all creatures made subject to us will be
     experienced, and a care felt in us that we do not lessen the
     sweetness of life in the animal creation which the great
     Creator intends for them under our government ...

        John Woolman

45   There have always been and still are many Church[people],
     both lay and ordained, who have seen it as part of their
     Christian profession to work for animal welfare. I want to
     offer my support to the RSPCA because without their
     constant vigilance and the devoted work of their Officers and
     Inspectors the level of unnecessary animal suffering in this

country would be so much higher. Animals, as part of God's creation, have rights which must be respected. It behoves us always to be sensitive to their needs and to the reality of their pain.

Donald Coggan

46 We may pretend to what religion we please; but cruelty is atheism. We may make our boast of Christianity; but cruelty is infidelity. We may trust to our orthodoxy; but cruelty is the worst of heresies.

Humphry Primatt

47 I expect to pass through this world but once; any good thing therefore that I can do, or any kindness that I can show to any fellow-creature, let me do it now; let me not defer or neglect it, for I shall not pass this way again.

Stephen Greller

48 But is it true that Death is the lord of any man or woman or child; of any beast or any insect; of any tree or flower? No. Death did not make them ... We wait for the Deliverer of these bodies from their aches and torments; we wait for the day when Christ shall set them free from the bondage of death; when he shall make them like his glorious body. And as we hope for ourselves, so we hope for all those creatures who not for their own fault have been made subject to misery and death, who are not sinful as we have been.

F. D. Maurice

Appendix 2

Guide to Sources and Further Reading on Animals and Spirituality

Acton, H. B., 'The Ethical Importance of Sympathy', *Philosophy*, vol. XXX, no. 112, January 1955, pp. 62–66.
A remarkable article in itself and as an anticipation of later work on animals. Argues that sympathy is 'a fundamental requirement for morality', and that sympathy requires that 'every sentient being shall *count* [morally] ...' (p. 66; author's emphasis).

Agius, Ambrose, *God's Animals*, Catholic Study Circle for Animal Welfare 1970.
Extracts 11 and 20 in Appendix 1 are taken from Cardinal Heenan's 'Foreword' on animal rights on p. 3, and from a letter by St Catherine of Siena, p. 43.

Allchin, A. M., *The World is a Wedding: Explorations in Christian Spirituality*, Darton, Longman and Todd 1987.
Cites and discusses Celano's account of St Francis of Assisi (pp. 85f.) an extract of which is reproduced in the Service for Animal Welfare.

Allchin, A. M., and de Waal, Esther (eds), *Threshold of Light: Prayers and Praises from the Celtic Tradition*, Darton, Longman and Todd, 1986.
A short selection of Celtic prayers some of which have an eco- or animal theme.

Allchin, A. M., and others, *Francis Hugh Maycock: A Tribute*, SLG Press 1981.
For extract 19 in Appendix 1, originally from Maycock's 'Borneo Diary', see pp. 20–21.

Anon, *Clemency to Brutes: The substance of two sermons preached on Shrove-Sunday with a particular view to dissuade from that species of cruelty annually practised in England, the throwing of cocks*, R. and J. Dodsley 1761.
One of the very earliest recorded English sermons against animal cruelty, specifically the sport of cock-throwing (throwing sticks at cocks tied to a post). Concludes with this delightful irony: '... were the Scriptures therefore so much in our minds as they ought to be, the bird which roused Saint Peter to repentance would on this occasion be considered as an alarm to ourselves' (p. 30).

Athanasius, St (*c.*296–377), *Contra Gentes and De Incarnatione*, ed and trs by R. W. Thompson, Clarendon Press 1971.
Extract 34 in Appendix 1, lines from which appear also in 'Celebrating the Creatures', can be found on pp. 117 and 115.

Attwater, Donald, *St John Chrysostom*, Catholic Book Club 1960.
For lines cited in the Introduction and the Service for Animal Welfare, see pp. 59–60. Attwater, unfortunately, does not give an exact reference for the lines.

Arluke, Arnold, and Sanders, Clinton R., *Regarding Animals*, Temple University Press 1996.
Provides sociological insights into human-animal relationships. The essay on the Nazis' apparent friendliness to animals is misleading, however. The view that 'in Nazi Germany disregard for human life was coupled with a deep concern for animals' (p. 164) utterly misses the point that the Nazis elevated social Darwinism – as exemplified by certain 'pure' animal species – to the detriment of other human and non-

human species. Despite the propaganda about animal welfare, Nazi experiments on animals were as horrific as their experiments on humans.

Baker, John Austin, *The Foolishness of God*, Darton, Longman and Todd 1970.
A classic of spirituality and theology. I have used his line (p. 406) about the crucified Christ as the only accurate picture of God in my 'Vigil for All Suffering Creatures'.

—, Sermon preached in York Minster (28 September 1986), *Animal Christian Concern News*, Winter 1986.
Few bishops have preached a more powerful sermon on reverence for life; extract 18 in Appendix 1.

—, *The Faith of a Christian*, Darton, Longman and Todd 1996.
A strongly incarnational defence of Christian faith and spirituality inclusive of concern for animals; see pp. 138–42.

Baker, Steve, *Picturing the Beast: Animals, Identity and Representation*, Manchester University Press and St Martin's Press 1993.
An important work on how 'animals figure in our thinking about human identity' (p. x) and the legacy this has left within our present culture. Baker, sadly, does not address the dominant theological ways of construing animals and their cultural significance, but he shows why such a work is essential if theology is to begin to critically review its understanding of animals.

Barth, Karl, *Church Dogmatics*, vol. III (4 parts), *The Doctrine of Creation*, ed by G. W. Bromiley and T. F. Torrance, T. & T. Clark 1958–61.
Despite his humanocentric perspectives on creation, Barth's theology constitutes a seedbed for creative revisionist theology in the area of animals. The lines used in 'A Vigil for All Suffering Creatures' are from *CD* III/3, p.301; cited and discussed in Fiddes, p. 224.

—, *The Faith of the Church: A Commentary on the Apostle's Creed According to Calvin's Catechism*, ed by Jean-Louis Leuba, trs by Gabriel Vahanian, Fontana Books 1960.
Source for Barth's view that animals also praise God, pp. 23f. However, Barth also appears to endorse the contrary view, see CD III/2, p. 143, where he writes of how 'we know nothing' of how creation gives thanks.

Basil the Great, St (*c*.330–79) *see* Torrance, T.F.

Bekoff, Marc, with Meaney, Carron A. (eds), *Encyclopedia of Animal Rights and Animal Welfare*, Greenwood Press 1998.
Contains numerous articles on religion and animals, and Alison A. Taylor and Hank Davis' entry on 'Memorial Services for Animal Research Subjects', pp. 223–25.

Birch, Charles, and Vischer, Lukas, *Living with the Animals: The Community of God's Creatures*, World Council of Churches 1997.
A very welcome addition to WCC publications. Offers two short but succinct and perceptively theological discussions on Christianity and animal ethics.

Blake, William (1757–1827).
Extract 42 in Appendix 1 is from his poem 'Auguries of Innocence', written about 1803.

Bonaventure, St (1221–74), *The Soul's Journey to God*, trs and intro by Ewert Cousins, Classics of Western Spirituality, SPCK 1979.
Lines from pp. 76–77 and 67–68 are reproduced as extract 36 in Appendix 1.

Bonhoeffer, Dietrich, *Letters and Papers from Prison*, The Enlarged Edition, SCM Press 1971.
The quotation in 'A Vigil for All Suffering Creatures' is from the letter of 16 July 1944, p. 361; cited and discussed in Fiddes, p. 2.

Bouyer, Louis, *Rite and Man: The Sense of the Sacral and Christian Liturgy*, trs by M. Joseph Costelloe, Burns and Oates and University of Notre Dame Press 1963.
A fine work defending the view that Christian rites draw upon 'natural rites' and a sense of 'natural sacredness'. The following two lines illustrate the thrust of the argument: 'As we are discovering today, sacredness is not some secondary, artificial adjunct to humanity as such. There is no humanity that does not, at least, remotely proceed from it' (p. 12).

—, *Eucharist: Theology and Spirituality of the Eucharistic Prayer*, trs by Charles Underhill Quinn, University of Notre Dame Press 1968.
A majesterial work on the development of eucharistic theology. I have used his selection from the Seventh Book of the Apostolic Constitutions (see pp. 130–31) in my Introduction to my 'Eucharistic Prayers for All Creatures'.

Bratton, Susan Power, *Christianity, Wilderness and Wildlife: The Original Desert Solitaire*, Associated University Presses 1993.
An excellent attempt to rediscover the 'wilderness' motif within the Christian tradition, but its conclusions indicate an instrumentalist understanding of nature. For example: '... we have to decide when we should harvest it [wild nature] and when we shouldn't' (p. 311). The idea that wild animals specifically are there to be 'harvested' is part of the problem rather than part of the solution.

Broome, Arthur, 'Prospectus of the SPCA', 25 June 1824, *RSPCA Records*, vol. II, (1823–26).
Makes clear the Christian inspiration for the founding of the RSPCA.

Brown, Peter, *The Body and Society: Men, Women and Sexual Renunciation in Early Christianity*, Faber and Faber 1988.
Though predominantly concerned with sexuality, the book

paints a picture of early Christianity disturbingly incapable of coming to terms with the flesh with knock-on implications for all fleshly creatures. Vegetarianism, for example, became part of an extreme asceticism called 'Encratism' (from *enkrateia*, 'continence'): '... for the eating of meat was held to link human beings to the wild, carnivorous nature of animals, as intercourse linked them to the sexual nature of brute beasts' (p. 93). Given this train of thought, we should not perhaps be surprised that ethical vegetarianism was hardly on the agenda.

Budge, Ernest A. Wallis (ed and trs), *The Wit and Wisdom of the Christian Fathers of Egypt* (Syrian version of the *Apophthegmata Patrum*), OUP 1934.
The book has yet to be written about the Desert Fathers and animals. But of the many stories about animals, perhaps the most remarkable collected here is that of a brother seen 'praying and entreating the Lord that the wild animals might be at peace with him. And after the prayer a panther which was suckling her young was found by him, and that brother went down upon his knees and sucked with them' (p. 191). See also Thomas Merton, *The Wisdom of the Desert: Sayings from the Desert Fathers of the Fourth Century* [1961], Sheldon Press 1974, and the saying of St Anthony that 'My book ... is the nature of created things, and any time I want to read the words of God, the book is before me' (p. 62).

Cadoux, C. J., *Catholicism and Christianity: A Vindication of Progressive Protestantism*, Foreword by J. Vernon Bartlett, Allen and Unwin 1928.
For extract 8 in Appendix 1 see p. 629. Cadoux was one of a number of Congregationalist theologians to grasp the importance of the animal issue. He was also a committed vegetarian, see his 'Is the Vegetarian Right?' in *The Vegetarian Messenger and Health Review*, October/November 1942, pp. 90f. (based on an address to the Leeds Vegetarian Society, 12 April 1942). Cadoux assembled a mass of material for a book on human duties to animals which sadly he was unable to complete. If finished, his work might have been one of the most important

attempts to integrate animal ethics into systematic theology. I am grateful to Elaine Kaye for these references. See her excellent biography, *C. J. Cadoux: Theologian, Scholar and Pacifist*, Edinburgh University Press 1988.

Calvin, John (1509–64), *Commentaries*, ed and trs by J. Haroutunian with L. P. Smith, The Library of Christian Classics, SCM Press 1958.
Volume XXII, p. 329, is my source for Calvin's statement about obligations to animals cited in 'A Service for Animal Welfare'.

Catherine of Siena, St (1347–80) *see* Agius, Ambrose

Celano *see* Allchin, A.M., *The World is a Wedding*

Chapouthier, Georges, and Nouet, Jean-Claude (eds), *The Universal Declaration of Animal Rights: Comments and Intentions*, Ligue Française des Droits de l'Animal 1998.
A French contribution to the debate about animal rights based on the Universal Declaration of Animal Rights originally promulgated in Paris in 1978. The revised Declaration is based on 'rational biocentrism or extended humanism' and its articles are weaker than before. A great pity that the book did not engage with the tradition of theologically-based rights. I doubt whether any form of humanism, enlightened or otherwise, can provide an adequate basis for animal rights. Regarding animal burials, Article 3.3 of the Declaration stipulates that 'A dead animal must be treated with decency' (p. 80).

Chrysostom, St John (c.347–407) *see* Attwater, Donald

Clarke, Paul Barry, and Linzey, Andrew (eds), *Dictionary of Ethics, Theology and Society*, Routledge 1996.
Contains two ground breaking entries on 'Creation' and 'Covenant' by Daniel W. Hardy; also entries by myself on, *inter alia*, 'animal rights', 'cruelty', 'ecotheology', 'farming', 'hunting', 'vegetarianism', 'vivisection', and 'zoos'.

Cochrane, Charles Norris, *Christianity and Classical Culture: A Study of Thought and Action from Augustus to Augustine*, OUP 1944.
Impressive account of the history of the Logos doctrine.

Coggan, Donald, 'Presidential Message to the Annual General Meeting of the RSPCA', *RSPCA Today*, no. 22, July 1977, p. 1.
Source for extract 45 in Appendix 1.

Conn, Eileen, and Stewart, James (eds), *Visions of Creation*, Foreword by Matthew Fox, Godsfield Press 1995.
A new eco-spiritual collection which contains Richard Woods' defence of Aquinas, pp. 54–63. He argues that Aquinas 'does not license us to do as we wish with nature' (p. 62). How Woods can square this positive reading with the actual words of Aquinas that '[i]t is not wrong for man to make use of them [animals], either by killing or in any other way whatever' (*Summa Contra Gentiles*, Third Book, Part II, ch. CXII), I do not know. Doubtless, Aquinas, like all great thinkers, can be read in different ways and encompass divergent emphases, but Woods' essay, like others, is an unwise attempt at Catholic revisionist theology. Much better to begin by frankly confronting what Aquinas got wrong.

Conner, David, 'Making Sense of Prayer' in Andrew Linzey and Peter J. Wexler (eds), *Fundamentalism and Tolerance: An Agenda for Theology and Society*, Bellew Publishing 1991, pp. 61–71.
A profound essay relating prayer to moments of illumination and insight as the work of God the Spirit within us.

Cooper, Nigel, *Wildlife in Church and Churchyard: Plants, Animals and their Management*, Church of England Council for the Care of Churches/Church House Publishing 1995.
An attempt to show how churches and parishes can be conservation-friendly but its section on animals, 'Wanted and

Unwanted Wildlife', pp. 34–40, is wholly inadequate and mostly endorses the common killing of animals. The section should be revised to include information about the non-lethal methods of control available, and, most importantly, some serious theological discussion of the worth of sentient creatures. Altogether a missed opportunity wholly indicative of the lack of attention given to animals at the heart of the inner structures of the Church of England.

Cox, Harvey, *The Feast of Fools: A Theological Essay on Festivity and Fantasy*, Harper and Row 1969.
   A brilliant defence of the social, moral and political signifi-cance of fantasy, festivity and ritual. 'The question we should be asking should run like this: Given the fact that our polis, the human community, needs a company of dreamers, seers, servants and jesters in its midst, where shall this company come from?' (p. 96).

Cummings, E. E (1894–1962).
   'i thank You God for most this amazing' from *Complete Poems 1904–1962* by E. E. Cummings, ed by George J. Firmage.
   Reprinted by permission of W. W. Norton & Company. Copyright © 1991 by the Trustees for the E. E. Cummings Trust and George James Firmage. Extract 38 in Appendix 1.

Danielou, Jean, *Prayer as a Political Problem*, ed and trs by J. R. Kirwan, Burns and Oates 1967.
   A pioneering work making connections between art, tech-nology, politics and spirituality.

DeGrazia, David, *Taking Animals Seriously: Mental Life and Moral Status*, CUP 1996.
   A heavyweight philosophical contribution critical of our current usage of animals. Chapters 4–7 survey and analyse the latest empirical evidence about animal consciousness, even touching upon apparent burial rituals in animals (p. 181).

Dekkers, Midas, *Dearest Pet: On Bestiality*, trs by Paul Vincent, Verso 1992.
A serious study of the psycho-sexual complexity of human/ animal companion relations, though I would have to add that Dekkers appears more welcoming of human overtures to the animal world that I am comfortable with. He also fails to adequately appreciate the cruelty and degradation to animals implicit in such encounters.

Dostoyevsky, Fyodor Mikhail, *The Brothers Karamanzov*, vol. 1, trs by David Magarshack, Penguin Books 1969.
For Father Zossima's extraordinary vision of inclusive love (part of which is included as extract 2 in Appendix 1), see p. 375.

Eaton, John, *The Circle of Creation: Animals in the Light of the Bible*, SCM Press 1995.
A useful reader-friendly introduction to biblical teaching on animals. Eaton's homely style masks substantial biblical scholarship.

Ecclestone, Alan, *Yes to God*, Darton, Longman and Todd 1975.
An impressive work offering a holistic vision of Christian spirituality. The lines from Charles Péguy (in the Introduction to 'Litanies for Animal Protection') can be found on p. 121. I am especially indebted to Ecclestone for his perceptive discussion of the relationship between spirituality and poetry, ch. 4, pp. 56–69.

Edwards, Denis, *Jesus the Wisdom of God: An Ecological Theology*, St Pauls 1995.
A superior presentation of eco-theology based on the notion of Jesus as the embodiment of the Hebrew Wisdom Tradition. Does not hesitate to include sentient creatures within its purview and its discussion is always insightful, see especially sections on the 'Intrinsic Value of All Creatures', 'Reverence

for Life' and 'Companions with Other Creatures in an Earth Community' in ch. 7 on 'Ecological Praxis', pp. 154ff. His definition of the 'Trinitarian God of Mutual Love and Fecundity' as the 'Center of Ecological Theology' (pp. 91ff.) is inspiring.

Eisenman, Robert, *James the Brother of Jesus*, vol. 1, *The Cup of the Lord*, Faber and Faber 1997.
Detailed examination of James' spirituality arguing that he was a vegetarian and that Paul's references to vegetarianism were 'a direct attack' on James' lifestyle (p. 261). Raises new questions about the extent of vegetarianism in the early church.

Eiesland, Nancy L., *The Disabled God: Towards a Liberatory Theology of Disability*, Foreword by Rebecca S. Chopp, Abingdon Press 1994.
A very fine essay on the implications of embodiment for theology and specifically the way in which the disabled have been marginalized by church practices. Many of her insights about 'the disabled God' (pp. 98f.) have equal relevance for our exclusion of animals.

Elder, John, *Imagining the Earth: Poetry and the Vision of Nature* [1986], The University of Georgia Press, second edition 1996.
A fine, closely argued work defending the primacy of poetic imagination in understanding nature. Ch.1, 'The Covenant of Loss' begins by exploring the poetic sense of our disharmony with nature and other creatures (pp. 7–23).

Eliot, T. S. (1888–1965), *Murder in the Cathedral*, Faber and Faber 1935.
Contains his memorable lines about creatures praising God (see pp. 92–3), some of which are included in 'A Service for Animal Welfare' by permission of the publisher.

Enright, D. J., and Rawlinson, David, (eds), *The Oxford Book of Friendship*, OUP 1992.
Contains an inspiring section, pp. 262–84, celebrating our friendship with animals.

Everett, Robert A., 'A Litany for Animals'.
A responsive prayer for animals from the Service for Animal Rights, 28 April 1985, at Emanuel United Church of Christ, New Jersey. Extract 14 in Appendix 1.

Fabre-Vassas, Claudine, *The Singular Beast: Jews, Christians and the Pig*, trs by Carol Volk, Columbia University Press 1997.
A fascinating, if disturbing, account of the history of cultural and religious conceptions of this much derided creature. I am indebted to Fabre-Vassas for the fact that in Agrigente the flagellation of Christ is still celebrated every 10 September by a massive pig slaughter (p. 256) and details of other sub-Christian rituals.

Fiddes, Paul S., *The Creative Suffering of God*, Clarendon Press 1988.
A great work of constructive modern theology which explores the idea of divine passibility. Scholarly, erudite and full of insight. His book helped inspire my 'Vigil for All Suffering Creatures' and I have used his pithy quotations from Jüngel, Moltmann, Tillich, Barth and Bonhoeffer at the start of the Vigil to help stimulate thought about the meaning of the Cross.

Francis of Assisi, St, *The Little Flowers, Mirror of Perfection, and St Bonaventure's Life*, intro by Hugh McKay, postscript by Eric Doyle, Everyman's Library, Dent 1973.
Ch. CXIV, p. 290, is the source for the story of St Francis and the Emperor reproduced as extract 5 in Appendix 1.

Gerwolls, Marilyn K., and Labott, Susan M., 'Adjustment to the Death of a Companion Animal', *Anthrozoos*, vol. VIII, no. 3, 1994, pp. 172–87.
The results 'indicated that, with few exceptions, the grief experience associated with a companion animal is similar to that with the loss of a significant human', and also that the 'adjustment process, although similar to that experienced when a human dies, may be hindered by a lack of social support and opportunities for healthy confiding in others' (p.172). These results underline the need for pastoral support from the churches and the appropriateness of liturgies for animal burial.

Gompertz, Lewis, *Moral Inquiries on the Situation of Man and Brutes* [1824], ed and intro by Charles Magel, Mellen Animal Rights Library Series, Edwin Mellen Press 1997.
One of the early philosophical defences of animals by the Jewish thinker who followed Arthur Broome as secretary of the SPCA. Magel's excellent introduction puts Gompertz in context and explains the contemporary relevance of his work.

Gosse, Gerald H., and Barnes, Michael J., 'Human Grief Resulting from the Death of a Pet', *Anthrozoos*, vol. VII, no. 2, 1994, pp. 103–12.
One of the many recent studies examining the effects of the loss of companion animals.

Graves, Robert (1895–1985), 'In the Wilderness' from his *Collected Poems*, Cassell 1975.
Perhaps the finest poem about Christ and animals ever written. Extract 10 in Appendix 1.

Gray, William, 'The Myth of the Word Discarnate', *Theology*, vol. 88, 722, March 1985, pp. 112–17.
A brilliant, logical defence of the materiality of the Logos.

Gregory Nazianzen, St (330–89), *Selected Poems*, trs and intro by John McGuckin, SLG Press 1986. © The Community of the Sisters of the Love of God 1986.
For extract 1 in Appendix 1 from his poem 'Hymn to God', see p. 7.

Greller, Stephen *see* Sykes, William G.D.

Grou, Jean, *Manual for Interior Souls*, Burns, Oates and Washbourne 1892.
A classic of 'otherwordly' spirituality. Most disturbing is ch. 5, 'On the violence we must use towards ourselves', pp. 25–31.

Gustafson, James M., *Intersections: Science, Theology and Ethics*, The Pilgrims Press 1996.
An oddly inconclusive work given Gustafson's earlier critique of theological humanism in *Theology and Ethics* (1981). For example, he argues that: 'Theology *per se* has no independent access to the patterns and processes of nature' (p. 109) which seems to obscure the fact that theology does offer a radically different view of nature, even a critique of it. I fear the book, like so much else written on theology and science, simply gives too much away.

Hammarskjöld, Dag, *Markings*, Foreword by W. H. Auden, trs by W. H. Auden and Leif Sjoberg, Faber and Faber 1964.
Notes and diary entries which became a classic of spirituality when published after the author's death. Not to be overlooked is the moving 'Elegy for my Pet Monkey' (p. 179).

Hardy, Daniel W., *God's Ways with the World: Thinking and Practising Christian Faith*, T. & T. Clark 1996.
Contains his demanding and insightful essay, 'Christ and Creation', on how we should 'do justice to creation and Christ, to take both seriously as mediating the presence of God' (p. 120).

Hardy, Thomas (1840–1928), *The Complete Poems*, ed by James Gibson, The New Wessex Edition, Macmillan 1976. Source for 'Compassion: An Ode' (pp. 822–23), reproduced as extract 30 in Appendix 1. The piece was written in celebration of the Centenary of the RSPCA on 22 January 1924. Hardy wrote many fine poems on the theme of human neglect of animals and actively supported the work of humanitarian organizations; see, for example, Martin Seymour-Smith, *Hardy*, Bloomsbury 1994, pp. 643–45.

Hart, John, *The Spirit of the Earth: A Theology of the Land*, Paulist Press 1984. A fascinating discussion of 'the land motif' in, *inter alia*, the Hebrew Bible. For extract 26 in Appendix 1, see p. 81.

Hastings, Adrian, *The Shaping of Prophecy: Passion, Perception and Practicality*, Geoffrey Chapman 1995. Contains his remarkable sermon on Jesus' entry into Jerusalem on an ass (pp. 175–77), from which extract 28 in Appendix 1 is taken.

Heenan, Cardinal *see* Agius, Ambrose

Holland, Alan, and Johnson, Andrew (eds), *Animal Biotechnology and Ethics*, Chapman and Hall 1998. Contains Michael Banner's essay defending his 1995 Report on the ethics of the genetic modification of farm animals. Curiously, despite his claim that his Report 'shows itself to be aware of what might be termed the embeddedness of questions in metaphysical and moral theories' (p. 325), his essay and the Report as a whole show little cognisance of fundamental theological objections to genetic modification. Indeed, his emphasis on cost/benefit analyses, not to mention his unsupported claim that genetic manipulation 'may actually result in an improvement [for the animals concerned]' (p. 337) preclude wider debate. The unaddressed theological question goes like this: Is it right to genetically alter the God-given lives of sentient individuals in order to make them bigger and better laboratory tools or meat machines? Even in terms of cost/benefit analysis, I have yet to read a serious piece which questions whether humans themselves benefit from a view of animals as genetically manipulable commodities.

Hopkins, Gerard Manley (1844–89).
Extract 22 in Appendix 1 is from his poem 'God's Grandeur'.

Hume, C. W., *The Status of Animals in the Christian Religion*, Universities Federation for Animal Welfare 1957. The animal blessings from the *Rituale Romanum* are discussed on pp. 95–98.

Irvine, Christopher (ed), *Celebrating the Easter Mystery: Worship Resources for Easter and Pentecost*, Foreword by Richard Harries, Mowbray 1996.
A fine resource book with new liturgies and commentaries. My only sadness is that despite the many implicit indications that Easter is a feast of the transfiguration of all creation, the liturgies themselves make none of this explicit.

Isaac the Syrian, St (*c.*347–438) *see* Lossky, Vladimir

John Paul II, Pope, Message on 'Reconciliation' (delivered at Assisi, 12 March 1982), *L'Osservatore Romano*, 29 March 1982, pp. 8–9.
Source for extract 6 in Appendix 1.

—, *Ecology and Faith*, ed by Ancilla Dent, Arthur James 1997.
Although Pope John Paul II has mentioned ecology (and sometimes animals) the total effect of this book (39 pages) only reinforces the sense that these issues have been peripheral to his teaching.

Johnson, Elizabeth A., *Women, Earth and Creator Spirit*, 1993 Madeleva Lecture in Spirituality, Paulist Press 1993. One of the many emerging eco-feminist writings. Whilst rightly rejecting a 'hierarchical, two-tiered view' of the world

(p. 40), Johnson makes the mistake of many ecologists in lumping animals together with 'the earth' as if our relations with all earth-forms should be identical. Notwithstanding the beauty and spiritual significance of 'earth relations', what ecologists desperately need is a sufficient grasp of the spirituality of specifically human/animal relationships.

Jones, Helen E., 'Animal Protection and the Church', *Bulletin of the National Catholic Society for Animal Welfare* (USA), March 1967, pp. 6–7.
An historically significant critique of church indifference to animals based on an address to the World Congress of the World Federation for the Protection of Animals, 10 October 1966. Subsequently the NCSWA forwent its specifically Catholic identity and became the (now International) Society for Animal Rights.

Julian of Norwich, *Showings*, trs and intro by Edmund Collage and James Walsh, Paulist Press 1978.
For the passages concerning Julian's famous vision about the hazel-nut and about all creatures suffering with Christ reproduced as extracts 4 and 29 in Appendix 1 see pp. 130–31 and 210.

Jung, C. G., *Memories, Dreams, Reflections* [1961], ed by Aniela Jaffre, trs by Richard and Clara Winston, Fontana Books 1967.
Contains his early reflections on the evil of predation, pp. 76–77, and his rejection of traditional Christian views of animals, pp. 85–89. Jungian spirituality is well placed to accommodate insights about the ethical status of animals.

Jüngel, Eberhard, *God as the Mystery of the World*, T. & T. Clark 1983.
The lines used in 'A Vigil for All Suffering Creatures' are from p. 363; cited and discussed in Fiddes, p. 150.

Kean, Hilda, *Animal Rights: Political and Social Change in Britain since 1800*, Reaktion Books 1998.
Despite the title, the book is really a history of the humanitarian movement since the nineteenth century. Focusses on Methodism, pp. 13–38, to the neglect of other Christian traditions, but is a superbly insightful history. Narrates the story of the Brown Dog Memorial in Battersea, pp. 153–56.

King, Ursula, *Spirit of Fire: The Life and Vision of Teilhard de Chardin*, Orbis 1996.

—, *Christ in All Things: Exploring Spirituality with Teilhard de Chardin*, Orbis and SCM Press 1997.
Moving, if rather uncritical, accounts of his evolutionary christocentric spiritual vision. For some of us, it is deeply puzzling how de Chardin managed to see such spiritual power in matter but little, if any, in living creatures as such.

Kowalski, Gary, *The Souls of Animals*, Stillpoint Publishing 1991.
Meditations on the spiritual power of animals by a Unitarian Universalist minister.

LaChance, Albert J., and Carroll, John E. (eds), *Embracing Earth: Catholic Approaches to Ecology*, Orbis 1994.
Some excellent pioneering essays – such as 'Christ the Ecologist' by John Carroll, 'Fruit of the Earth, Fruit of the Vine' by Charles Cummings, and 'An Eco-Prophetic Parish?' by Paula Gonzalez. But it is amazing that animals get so little a look in – until the end. An unacknowledged 'prayer for animals' is reproduced on the final page (276) which is in fact a prayer of Albert Schweitzer. An impressive volume but one which sadly testifies to the current eco/animal split.

Lawson, Chris, *Some Quaker Thoughts on Animal Welfare*, Quaker Social Responsibility and Education 1985.
My source for passages from Woolman (*Journal* 1772); extracts 24 and 44 in Appendix 1 are both from pp. 2–3.

Lee, Laura and Martyn, *Absent Friend*, Henston Books 1992.
A factual and sympathetic guide for people suffering from the loss of a companion animal.

Lenten Triodion, trs by Mother Mary and Bishop Kallistos, Faber and Faber 1978.
Contains the lines about all sentient creatures suffering with Christ from the Matins of Holy Saturday according to the Byzantine Rite reproduced in my 'Memorial Prayers for Animals'. I have slightly modernized the language.

Linzey, Andrew, *Animal Rights: A Christian Assessment*, SCM Press 1976.
My first book which heralded the modern animal rights movement.

—, *Christianity and the Rights of Animals*, SPCK and Crossroad 1987.
A defence of 'theos-rights', i.e. God's rights as Creator to have what is created treated with respect.

—, 'The Theological Basis of Animal Rights', *The Christian Century*, 9 October 1991, pp. 906–9.
Defends human uniqueness as the basis for animal rights.

—, *Animal Theology*, SCM Press and University of Illinois Press 1994.
A systematic exploration of theological principles and their application.

—, 'C. S. Lewis's Theology of Animals', *Anglican Theological Review*, vol. LXXX, no. 1, Winter 1998, pp. 60–81.
An analysis of Lewis' pioneering contribution to a theological understanding of animals.

—, 'Unfinished Creation: The Moral and Theological Significance of the Fall', *EcoTheology*, no. 4, 1998, pp. 20–26.
My defence of the doctrine of the Fall and its implications for our understanding of creation.

—, *Animal Gospel*, Hodder and Stoughton 1998.
A pastoral and evangelical sequel to *Animal Theology* (1994).

Linzey, Andrew, and Cohn-Sherbok, Dan, *After Noah: Animals and the Liberation of Theology*, Cassell and Crossroad 1997.
An exploration of the resources within Judaism and Christianity for a positive view of animals. Ch. 6, 'How Animals can Liberate Jewish and Christian Theology', pp. 117–37, suggests that animals can help release our respective theologies from idolatry, humanism, and hubris.

Linzey, Andrew, and Regan, Tom (eds), *Compassion for Animals: Readings and Prayers*, SPCK and Crossroad 1988.
The natural counterpart to this volume, now sadly out of print. I have included some of the best pieces in Appendix 1 of additional prayers and readings.

—, (eds), *Animals and Christianity: A Book of Readings*, SPCK and Crossroad 1988.
A selection of readings for and against animals by classical and modern thinkers including Augustine, Bonaventure, Aquinas, Descartes, Calvin, Barth, Tillich and Schweitzer.

—, (eds), *Song of Creation: An Anthology of Poems in Praise of Animals*, Marshall Pickering 1988.
Source for poems by Rossetti, Wordsworth, Blake, Hopkins and Tennyson included in Appendix 1.

Linzey, Andrew, and Yamamoto, Dorothy (eds), *Animals on the Agenda: Questions about Animals for Theology and Ethics*, SCM Press and University of Illinois Press 1998.
An encyclopaedic volume addressing basic theological questions about animals. Contains Richard Bauckham's two essays on 'Jesus and Animals: (1) What did he teach?' and '(2) What did he practice?', pp. 33–48, 49–60; and James Gaffney's essay on 'Can Catholic Morality Make Room for Animals?',

pp. 100–12, which discusses Newman's remarkable sermon on the Christ-like innocence of animals.

Lossky, Vladimir, *The Mystical Theology of the Eastern Church*, trs by members of the Fellowship of St Alban and St Sergius, James Clarke 1952.
See p. 111 for the extract from St Isaac the Syrian discussed in the Introduction. Lossky does not give a reference for the lines.

Low, Mary, *Celtic Christianity and Nature: Early Irish and Hebridean Traditions*, Edinburgh University Press 1996.
A fine survey. Brings out the Celtic fascination with birds – imaged as the 'souls of the righteous in the Tree of Life', pp. 113f.

Manning, Aubrey, and Serpell, James (eds), *Animals and Human Society: Changing Perspectives*, Routledge 1994.
A variable collection but contains Andreas-Holger Maehle's excellent essay on 'Cruelty and Kindness to the "Brute Creation"' (pp. 81–105) which illustrates how modern reformers are indebted to early Christian debates about animals.

Marvin, Frederic Rowland, *Christ Among the Cattle*, J. O. Wright and Co. 1899.
An early American sermon against cruelty preached in the First Congregational Church, Portland, Oregon. Takes up the motif of Christ born in a stable in order to establish justice for all creatures.

Mascall, E. L., *Corpus Christi: Essays on the Church and the Eucharist*, Longmans 1965.
One of the few conservative theologians to grasp the significance of the eucharist for the entire created order; see 'The Eucharist and the Order of Creation', pp. 173–82.

Maurice, F. D., *Sermons Preached in Country Churches*, Macmillan and Co. 1880.
Extracts 7 and 48 in Appendix 1 are from the sermons on

'The Gift of Hearing' and 'Suffering and Glory', pp. 14 and 345–47.

Maximus, St (580–662), *Selected Writings*, trs and notes by George C. Berthold, intro by Jaroslav Pelikan, SPCK and Paulist Press 1985.
My source for Maximus on the Logos, pp.186f. and 'man as the microcosm' of creation, pp.196f. One day theologians will begin to appropriate Maximus' vision of the cosmic Christ for contemporary eco- and animal theology.

Maycock, Francis Hugh (1903–80) *see* Allchin, A.M., *Francis Hugh Maycock*

McDaniel, Jay B., *With Roots and Wings: Christianity in an Age of Ecology and Dialogue*, Orbis 1995.
An impressive statement of holistic spirituality drawn from a variety of multi-faith sources from a process theologian deeply interested in specifically animal issues.

McMichael, Ralph N. Jr., (ed), *Creation and Liturgy: Studies in Honor of H. Boone Porter*, The Pastoral Press 1993.
Another excellent collection on creation in the liturgical tradition with many thoughtful and pioneering essays. The final section in which Porter's hunting activities are lauded cannot but suggest a certain moral blindness.

Merton, Thomas, *No Man is an Island*, Burns and Oates 1955.
For extract 15 in Appendix 1, see p. 16.

—, *Seeds of Contemplation* [1949], Burns and Oates 1957.
See p.5 for lines used in 'A Liturgy for Animal Burial'. Merton was one of the spiritual figures of the twentieth century who also opposed animal cruelty, for example, see his contribution to *Unlived Life: A Manifesto Against Factory Farming*, Campaigners Against Factory Farming 1966, p. 16; extract in Linzey and Regan, *Compassion for Animals*, p. 50.

Milward, Peter, *Approach to Ecology*, annotated by Terutada Okada, Eihosa Books 1992.
Sympathetic Catholic discussion of ecology and animals by a Jesuit from Sophia University, Tokyo.

Moltmann, Jürgen, *The Crucified God*, SCM Press 1974.

—, *The Church in the Power of the Spirit*, SCM Press, 2nd edn 1992.
Vols 2 and 3 in Moltmann's great trilogy. The lines used in 'A Vigil for All Suffering Creatures' are from p. 277 of *The Crucified God* and p. 60 of *The Church in the Power of the Spirit*; cited and discussed in Fiddes, pp. 4, 85.

Moule, C. F. D., *The Birth of the New Testament* [1962], A. & C. Black 1971.
Classic account of the growth of *inter alia* christological doctrine.

Newman, John Henry, 'The Crucifixion' [1842], *Parochial and Plain Sermons*, 8 vols, Rivingtons 1868, vol. vii.
Newman's impressive defence of the Christ-like innocence of animals. See pp. 136–37 for lines reproduced in 'A Vigil for All Suffering Creatures'.

Norton, Bryan G., Hutchins, Michael, Stevens, Elizabeth F., and Maple, Terry L. (eds), *Ethics on the Ark: Zoos, Animal Welfare and Wildlife Conservation*, Smithsonian Institute Press 1995.
A valuable collection of divergent views on the ethics of captivity. What the whole collection lacks, however, is a theological voice which defends animal liberty in the light of God's own blessing of animals to be as they are.

Paffard, Michael, *The Unattended Moment*, SCM Press 1976.
Collects and explores a range of numinous-like experiences found in classical and contemporary writers. The book is

suggestive of a wide range of spiritual experiences still largely ignored by the churches.

Page, Ruth, *God and the Web of Creation*, SCM Press 1996.
Contains a sympathetic section on animals, 'The Moral Standing of the Non-Human', pp. 131–52. My basic disagreement with Page is the way in which she espouses the 'web' (community or biotic based) model of creation in such a way that compromises the welfare or rights of individual sentients. Since I doubt whether she would subscribe to a wholly communitarian ethic in relation to human subjects it seems illogical to do so in the case of sentient animal subjects. I suggest that a more balanced theological view should be concerned with God's interest in individuals as well as community, but not community at the expense of sentient individuals within it.

Palmer, Martin, and Breuilly, Elizabeth, *After the Ark: Religious Understanding of Ourselves and Other Animals*, Forbes Publications 1996.
A pan religious resource book for schools. Inevitably rather slight but does contain some useful suggestions for activities, not least of all school assembly material for celebrating animals (pp. 84–85) and marking their death (pp. 90–91).

Péguy, Charles (1873–1924).
The lines used in the Introduction to 'Litanies for Animal Protection' are used without reference by Alan Ecclestone in *Yes to God*.

Pope, Alexander, 'Of Cruelty to Animals' [1713] in Rosalind Vallance (ed), *A Hundred English Essays*, Thomas Nelson and Sons 1950.
An early, pioneering essay against cruelty to animals. Extract 12 in Appendix 1 is from p. 159.

Primatt, Humphry, *The Duty of Mercy and the Sin of Cruelty to Brute Animals* [1776] ed with an intro by Andrew

Linzey, Mellen Animal Rights Library Series, Edwin Mellen Press 1999.
Perhaps the earliest systematic theological defence of animals. For extract 46 in Appendix 1, see p. 288.

Pottebaum, Gerard A., *The Rites of People: Exploring the Ritual Character of Human Experience* [1975], The Pastoral Press 1992.
An insightful discussion of the value of rituals. Ch. 6 on 'By Their Rites You Will Know Them', pp. 81–93, could well be appropriated as the theme of this volume.

Reiss, Michael J. and Straughan R., *Improving Nature? The Science and Ethics of Genetic Engineering*, CUP 1996.
In my view the attempt to genetically engineer nature poses the greatest threat, practically and theoretically, to the Christian doctrine of creation (see my *Animal Theology*, pp. 138–55). Sadly the chapter on 'Theological Concerns' (pp. 70–89) is wholly inadequate: more a survey of views than a connected argument.

Robson, Michael, *St Francis: The Legend and the Life*, Geoffrey Chapman 1997.
A sympathetic and scholarly biography of St Francis which does not overlook his radical view of creation and animals in particular, pp. 239–46. Argues, incidentally, that St Bonaventure explicitly endorsed an afterlife for animals (p. 245).

Rossetti, Christina (1830–94).
Extract 16 in Appendix 1 is from her poem 'To What Purpose this Waste?'

Rowlands, Mark, *Animal Rights: a Philosophical Defence*, Macmillan 1998.
An impressive new work which defends a secular contractarian theory of animal rights. In years' past, it would

have been thought inconceivable that a notion of an 'ethical contract' could be devised without reference to the God of the covenant, but here it is. Notwithstanding the excellence of this work, I look forward to the theological critique which will try to indicate the limitations of any purely humanocentric 'covenantal' basis for animal rights.

Salisbury, Joyce E., *The Beast Within: Animals in the Middle Ages*, Routledge 1994.
Those who hold that mediaeval attitudes to animals were far more positive than animal advocates have supposed will find serious contrary evidence in this book. Salisbury, a mediaevalist, is emphatic: 'Only in the late eighteenth and nineteenth centuries did we seem to have decided that humans and animals share feelings – thus concluding that humans should be careful of the feelings of animals' (p. 3).

Sargent, Tony, *Animal Rights and Wrongs: A Bibilical Perspective*, Hodder and Stoughton 1996.
Grapples with animal rights from a conservative evangelical standpoint.

Schmitt, Jean-Claude, *The Holy Greyhound: Guinefort, Healer of Children since the Thirteenth Century*, CUP 1983.
An impressive and careful study of the cult of the 'Greyhound Saint'. I am grateful to Benedicta Ward for this reference.

Schweitzer, Albert, *My Life and Thought: An Autobiography*, trs by C. T. Campion, Allen and Unwin 1933.
See pp. 279–80 for passage in 'A Vigil for All Suffering Creatures'. Schweitzer's thought has anticipated later eco- and animal sensitivity. The book has yet to be written which does justice to the range and complexity of his theological vision. Also much needed is a revised and updated collection of his works, especially his *Civilization and Ethics* (1923).

—, *Memoirs of Childhood and Youth*, Syracuse University Press 1997.
Source for Schweitzer's night-time prayer for animals (p. 37) reproduced as extract 31 in Appendix 1. I am grateful to Ara Barsam for this reference.

Smith, Abraham, *A Scriptural and Moral Catechism designed chiefly to lead the minds of the rising generation to the love and practice of mercy and to expose the horrid nature and exceeding sinfulness of cruelty to the dumb creation*, Richard Peart, 2nd edn 1833.
The 'Address to Ministers of Religion', pp. 50–56, is an early attempt to spell out to clergy their obligation to abjure cruelty.

Sorabji, Richard, *Animal Minds and Human Morals: The Origins of the Western Debate*, Duckworth 1993.
Shows how many of the supposedly 'modern' ideas about animal rights were in fact the subject of extensive debate among the ancients. Ch. 14 on the Christian tradition is very slight, and Augustine receives inordinate attention. Discusses St Basil the Great, pp. 203–4.

Spretnak, Charlene, *The Spiritual Dimension of Green Politics*, Bear and Company 1986.
The first of the 'Ten Key Values of the American Green Movement' (pp. 76–82) concerns 'the rights of nonhuman species', p. 78.

Spurgeon, Charles H., 'First Things First', *The Metropolitan Tabernacle Pulpit*, vol. XXXI (1885).
Source for Spurgeon's comments on companion animals, p. 559. I am grateful to Adrian Hastings for this reference.

Stefanatos, Joanne, *Animals and Man: A State of Blessedness*, Light and Life Publishing Company 1992.
An eccentric book, partly didactic, partly descriptive, written from an Orthodox Church perspective. Contains some unusual source material on the saints and animals, including

saints Aemeilians, Eleutherius, Hilarion, Mamas, and Theophil.

Styles, John, *The Animal Creation: Its Claim on our Humanity Stated and Enforced* [1839], ed and intro by Gary Comstock, Mellen Animal Rights Library Series, Edwin Mellen Press 1997.
A pioneering work of early zoophily detailing contemporary cruelties and providing a Christian critique. Comstock's fine introduction draws out the theological and philosophical emphases and provides a critical assessment.

Sykes, William G. D. (ed), *Visions of Faith: An Anthology of Reflections*, Marshall Pickering 1986.
A useful quarry for source material and especially helpful in opening out themes for discussion with students. Extract 47 in Appendix 1, attributed without further source to Stephen Greller, is from p. 188.

Teilhard de Chardin, Pierre, *Hymn of the Universe*, trs by Gerald Vann, Fontana Books 1974.
His lyrical poem about Christ and creation. A *tour de force* of spirituality. For extracts 32 and 43 in Appendix 1, see pp. 24–25 and 50–51.

Tennyson, Alfred, Lord (1809–92).
Extract 36 in Appendix 1 is from *In Memoriam*, liv.

Thoreau, Henry David, 'Walking' [1862] in *Civil Disobedience and other Essays*, Dover Publications 1993.
The opening lines of the essay on 'Walking' are memorable: 'I wish to speak a word for Nature, for absolute freedom and wildness, as contrasted with a freedom and culture merely civil, – to regard man as an inhabitant, or a part and parcel of nature, rather than a member of society' (p. 49). The book has yet to be written that explores the significance of Thorean spirituality for our relations with animals. I am grateful to Brian Klug for this reference.

Tillich, Paul, *Systematic Theology*, vol. I, *Reason and Revelation* and *Being and God* [1951], SCM Press 1978.
Source for the distinction between 'ecstatic' and 'formal' reason, pp. 53ff. I am grateful to Ara Barsam for this reference.

—, *Systematic Theology*, vol. II, *Existence and the Christ* [1957], SCM Press 1978.
For Tillich's speculations about incarnation in other non-human worlds, and for extract 33 in Appendix 1, see pp. 95–96. The lines used in 'A Vigil for All Suffering Creatures' are from p. 203; cited and discussed in Fiddes, p. 161.

Tolstoy, Leo, *Resurrection*, trs by Vera Traill, New American Library 1961.
The novel that begins with Tolstoy's vision of Springtime in creation marred by human sinfulness. For extract 25 in Appendix 1, see p. 9.

Torrance, T. F., *Theology in Reconstruction*, SCM Press 1965.
Discusses St Basil the Great's theology of the Spirit and creation. For extract 17 in Appendix 1, from *De Spiritu Sancto*, see pp. 220 and 222.

Turner, James, *Reckoning with the Beast: Animals, Pain and Humanity in the Victorian Mind*, The Johns Hopkins University Press 1980.
Provides a detailed account of the Christian founding of the RSPCA, pp. 43f.

van der Post, Laurens (1906–96)
The source of extract 35 in Appendix 1 is unknown.

Vanstone, W. H., 'On the Being of Nature', *Theology*, July 1997.
A pioneering essay anticipating eco- and animal concerns. For extract 39 in Appendix 1, see p. 283.

Ward, Keith, *The Concept of God*, Basil Blackwell 1974.
For extract 21 in Appendix 1, see pp. 222–24; also extract in
Linzey and Regan, *Animals and Christianity*, pp. 104–5.

Ware, Kallistos, *The Orthodox Way*, St Vladimir's Seminary
Press 1998.
Source for St Isaac's definition of spiritual intellect as 'simple
cognition', p. 48. I am grateful to Ara Barsam for this
reference.

Webb, Stephen H., *On God and Dogs: A Christian Theology
of Compassion for Animals*, OUP 1998.
An important new book arguing for the concept of divine
grace as a way of understanding our relationships with companion animals. Such relationships of apparent 'excess' mirror
the self-giving of God. In my 'Foreword', pp. ix–xii, I welcome
and praise the book whilst indicating some points of disagreement.

Wesley, John, *Sermons on Several Occasions*, 4 vols with
biographical note by J. Beecham, Wesleyan Conference
Office 1874.
Vol. ii contains his sermon, 'The General Deliverance', pp.
121–32, in which he espouses animal immortality. For extract
41 in Appendix 1, see p. 129. For Wesley's opposition to cruel
sports, see his entry for July 1756, *Journal* (standard edition),
Charles H. Kelley 1909, vol. 4, p. 176.

Whelen, Robert, Kirwan, Joseph, and Haffner, Paul, *The
Cross and the Rainforest: A Critique of Radical Green
Spirituality*, William B. Eerdmans 1996.
There is surely an important critique to be made of 'radical
green spirituality', but this is not it. Ch.3 on 'Greens and
Animals' by Joseph Kirwan is a polemic against the 'pagan'
animal rights movement (p. 112). In order to defend his
position, he makes use of Aquinas' view that friendship is
impossible with 'irrational' animals which will be embarrass-
ing to modern Thomists who have been trying hard to

rehabilitate Aquinas in animal discussions. Kirwan (former Principal of Plater College, Oxford) has probably done a service to traditionalists in spelling out precisely how unenlightened traditional teaching still is about animals.

Whitehouse, W. A., *The Authority of Grace: Essays in Response to Karl Barth*, ed by Ann Loades, T. & T. Clark 1981.
A deeply perceptive collection of essays on Barth, especially on the limitations of his doctrine of creation.

Wilberforce, Basil, 'The Foundation Stone' in *The Anti-Vivisection Review*, ed by L. Lind-af-Hagby, vol. I, 1909, pp. 52–55.
A sermon preached by the Archdeacon of Westminster, at a service for the Anti-Vivisection Congress at St John's Westminster, 11 July 1909. Powerful argument against cruelty which anticipates some modern theological themes. For example, on divine passibility: 'God is not, therefore, an onlooker from without upon the sufferings of the world, but a sharer from within. And there is not a pang in this suffering universe that does not pierce the heart of God before it reaches the consciousness of the individual sufferer' (p. 53).

Wilson, A. N., *Tolstoy*, Penguin Books 1989.
An awesome and deeply moving account of Tolstoy's life revealing a man of immense spirituality. Tolstoy's opposition to violence to animals as well as humans is prophetic and his analysis penetrating. He writes: 'Men of our time do not merely pretend to hate oppression, inequality, class distinction, and all kinds of cruelty not only to men but to animals ... they really do hate all this, but they do not know how to abolish it or cannot make up their minds to part with the system that supports it all but seems to them indispensable' (pp. 408–9).

Winter, Scott, 'All praise be yours' (based on St Francis of Assisi), from 'Liturgy of the Earth Mass on the Solemnity

of St Francis', 5 October 1986, Cathedral Church of St John the Divine, New York, pp. 1–2.
Source for extract in 'A Service for Animal Welfare'. The Cathedral Church in New York holds an annual service in celebration of the creatures.

Woolman, John (1720–72) *see* Lawson, Chris

Wordsworth, William (1770–1850).
Extract 39 in Appendix 1 is from his 'Lines composed a few miles above Tintern Abbey'.

Yarnold, G. D., *The Bread Which We Break*, OUP 1960.
A study of the eucharist arguing that it is an 'earthly foretaste' of cosmic renewal: ' ... the promise must also look to a future fulfilment in the world to come. It is only in the consummation of all things that the apostles receive their crowns, and the faithful their white robes; and that all may share eternally in the worship of heaven, and in the marriage supper of the Lamb' (pp. 75–76).

Notes

Publication details of works cited will be found in Appendix 2.

Introduction

1. Collected in Linzey and Regan, *Compassion for Animals*, p.34. The translation has been slightly modernized with inclusive language in mind.
2. Cited in Lossky, p.111.
3. Lossky, pp.111–12, my italics.
4. Cited in Attwater, pp.59–60.
5. Bauckham in Linzey and Yamamoto, p.38.
6. Ibid., p.46.
7. Moule, p.167.
8. Bonaventure, pp.254–55; 77, 67–68.
9. Ware, p.48; for the distinction between 'ecstatic' and 'formal' reasoning, and for an analysis of the different forms of knowledge, see Tillich, pp.53, 97–100.
10. Whitehouse, p.210.
11. Grou, pp.33, 159.
12. Athanasius, pp.23–25; discussed in Linzey and Cohn-Sherbok, p.101.
13. See Salisbury, p.175 and Jean-Claude Schmitt.
14. Kirwan in Whelan, Kirwan and Haffner, p.111.
15. Linzey 1994, esp. pp.45–61.
16. Linzey 1991, p.908.
17. Primatt, pp.5f.
18. Bouyer, pp.9, 11,27.
19. See ch.6, 'Animal Rights as Religious Vision', Linzey 1998.
20. See Sorabji.
21. See Linzey and Cohn-Sherbok.
22. Linzey in Linzey and Yamamoto, p. 3.

23. See Linzey 1987; also Heenan's landmark statement of 1970, his Foreword to Ambrose Agius' *God's Animals*, included as extract 11 in Appendix 1.
24. Pottebaum, p.81.

1. *Celebrating the Creatures*

1. Barth 1960, p.23.
2. Linzey and Cohn-Sherbok, p.12.
3. See Clark in Linzey and Yamamoto, pp.123–36.
4. See Linzey 1989.

2. *A Service for Animal Welfare*

1. See Turner, p.45.
2. Broome, p.203.
3. See Linzey,1994, p.19.
4. Ibid., pp.ix, 28–44.

3. *Eucharistic Prayers for All Creatures*

1. See Bouyer 1968, p.124; Linzey and Cohn-Sherbok, p.93.
2. Bouyer 1968, p.131; Linzey and Cohn-Sherbok, p.95.
3. Maximus, pp.196–97.
4. Linzey 1994, p.57.
5. Mascall, p.176.

4. *Covenanting with Animals*

1. Linzey 1987, pp.67ff, 154ff; Linzey and Cohn-Sherbok, pp.118, 133.
2. Spurgeon, p.559.
3. Webb, pp.xf. and my commentary.

5. *Liturgies for the Healing of Animals*

1. Linzey and Cohn-Sherbok, p.65.
2. Ibid., p.66; Bauckham in Linzey and Yamamoto, p.39.
3. See Bauckham, op.cit., for commentary, pp.33–38.
4. For commentary see ibid., pp.54–60.
5. Linzey and Cohn-Sherbok, pp.70–71.
6. Hume, and commentary, pp.94–98.

6. Litanies for Animal Protection

1. Linzey and Cohn-Sherbok, p.126.
2. Péguy, cited in Ecclestone, p.121.
3. Ibid., p.122.

7. A Vigil for All Suffering Creatures

1. Newman, p.137; discussed by Gaffney in Linzey and Yamamoto, pp.106ff.

8. Forms for the Blessing of Animals

1. Barth 1958, p.170.

9. A Liturgy for Animal Burial

1. Wesley, p.129.
2. Ibid., p.131.
3. See Gerwolls et al., pp.172–87.

10. Memorial Prayers for Animals

1. For details of the historical controversy, see Kean, pp.153–56.
2. See Taylor and Davis in Bekoff, pp.223–25.